GUIDANCE MONOGRAPH SERIES

SHELLEY C. STONE

BRUCE SHERTZER

Editors

GUIDANCE MONOGRAPH SERIES

The general purpose of Houghton Mifflin's Guidance Monograph Series is to provide high quality coverage of topics which are of abiding importance in contemporary counseling and guidance practice. In a rapidly expanding field of endeavor, change and innovation are inevitably present. A trend accompanying such growth is greater and greater specialization. Specialization results in an increased demand for materials which reflect current modifications in guidance practice while simultaneously treating the field in greater depth and detail than commonly found in textbooks and brief journal articles.

The list of eminent contributors to this series assures the reader expert treatment of the areas covered. The monographs are designed for consumers with varying familiarity to the counseling and guidance field. The editors believe that the series will be useful to experienced practitioners as well as beginning students. While these groups may use the monographs with somewhat different goals in mind, both will benefit from the treatment given to content areas.

The content areas treated have been selected because of specific criteria. Among them are timeliness, practicality, and persistency of the issues involved. Above all, the editors have attempted to select topics which are of major substantive concern to counseling and guidance personnel.

Shelley C. Stone

Bruce Shertzer

BEHAVIORAL COUNSELING

INITIAL PROCEDURES, INDIVIDUAL AND GROUP STRATEGIES

WILLIAM H. CORMIER
LOUISE S. CORMIER

WEST VIRGINIA UNIVERSITY

HOUGHTON MIFFLIN COMPANY · BOSTON

ATLANTA · DALLAS · GENEVA, ILL. · HOPEWELL, N.J. · PALO ALTO

ISBN: 0–395–200377

Library of Congress Catalog Card
Number: 74–11962

CONTENTS

LIST OF TABLES

LIST OF FIGURES

EDITORS' INTRODUCTION

Probably no contemporary approach to counseling has been as active and productive during the past decade as has the behavioral approach. Based solidly on learning theory, behavioral counseling views the counselor as functioning as an aid in the learning process who arranges conditions for the client to learn adaptive behavior which he can utilize to cope with his problems and concerns.

This monograph and its companion piece, *Behavioral Counseling: Operant Procedures, Self-Management Strategies, and Recent Innovations,* in Set VIII of the Guidance Monograph Series provide thorough and excellent coverage of the behavioral approach to individual and group counseling. The foundation, basic structure and application of behavioral counseling are explained clearly and in detail.

The Cormiers are to be congratulated for producing two scholarly monographs which are readable, timely and comprehensive. The texts are basic reading for anyone wishing to become familiar with behavioral counseling and the bibliographies provide extensive references for the reader who wishes to delve further into the research and practice of behavioral counseling.

SHELLEY C. STONE
BRUCE SHERTZER

AUTHORS' INTRODUCTION

This monograph will introduce the reader to the purpose, principles, procedures, and research associated with behavioral counseling. The initial procedures in behavioral counseling of problem identification and developing goals, as well as some individual and group strategies also are discussed. While a broad range of principles and procedures is described, the major procedures are illustrated with only a representative sample of research studies that depict a particular strategy. In this sense, the monograph can be considered as a collection of "hors-d'oeuvres" designed to increase the reader's understanding of behavioral counseling and to stimulate further investigation. The studies cited in this book were selected for their contribution to a particular strategy. Other pertinent studies, published and unpublished, could not be included because of the page limitation of the monograph.

In exploring the monograph, the reader will discover that behavioral counseling is based heavily on an empirical approach; the procedures are derived from cumulative evidence from an array of case studies and experimental evidence. As new procedures in behavioral counseling are developed, they are evaluated and modified on the basis of the empirical findings. It may well be that within the next decade some of the procedures described in this book may change as new studies are performed and new evidence is accumulated. Behavioral research has received widespread economic support, particularly in recent years. Stolz (1973) observed that the proportion of monetary support given over by the Clinical Research Branch of the National Institute for Mental Health for behavioral projects increased from 32 percent in 1967 to 54 percent in 1971. She concluded that this shift occurred primarily because behavioral researchers define their terms and interventions and are able to demonstrate "measurable and specifiable" outcomes (1973, p. 510).

The reader will also note that, in many instances, the terms "counseling" and "therapy" are used interchangeably and synonymously in this monograph. While one could argue for a complete and separate distinction between these two terms, many of the processes are similar. Some of the procedures illustrated in this book can and are being used by a variety of persons involved in the helping professions (e.g. counselors, social workers, psychologists).

In reflecting upon the writing process of this monograph, we would like to comment on some areas of personal appreciation and meaning. We appreciate the careful work of the monograph editors, Shelley Stone and Bruce Shertzer, who provided us with the opportunity to share our ideas and synthesize the significant ideas of others. We are indebted to our outstanding typist, Anne Drake, who worked with us quickly and efficiently under tight time pressures.

For a variety of personal and professional reasons, this book is dedicated to one who has a very special place in our hearts, Edward Hofler, C.S.P.

W. H. C.
L. S. C.

1

What Is Behavioral Counseling?

Behavioral counseling includes a variety of different procedures and strategies which are related to or based upon theories of learning. These procedures may be described by any of the following: contingency management, behavior therapy, behavioral counseling, behavior modification, functional analysis of behavior, experimental analysis of behavior, or applied behavior analysis. Therapy and counseling are used synonymously in this monograph because both terms involve similar processes which can be applied to the same settings and used with a variety of clients. The purpose of counseling is to change the client's overt and covert (cognitions, emotions, physiological states) responses. Also, environmental conditions contributing to an identified problem may need to be modified. Neither the behavior nor the environment can be overlooked in the change process, since these two events are related in a reciprocal manner; the behavior partially creates the environment which, in turn, influences the behavior. As Bandura stressed in his Presidential address at the American Psychological Association (1974), "To the oft-repeated dictum, change contingencies and you change behavior, should be added the reciprocal side, change behavior and you change the contingencies . . . since in everyday life this 'two-way control operates concurrently' [p. 866]." The focus of behavioral counseling may be an individual client, a group, an institution, or other environmental consequences. As Krasner and Ullmann (1965) have indicated, behavioral approaches to helping people encompass the total field of psychology relating to the control, change, or modification of human behavior.

The procedures and strategies developed by behavioral counselors are derived largely from experimental investigation. The results of experimental investigations of behavioral procedures provide a vast amount of *"cumulative evidence"* upon which present and future methods of treatment are utilized and modified. The principles of behavioral counseling are not new, but "what is new . . . is the *systematic evaluation* of how these principles affect the client [Lovaas, Koegel, Simmons, and Long, 1973, p. 164]." For the practitioner, this characteristic of behavioral counseling requires a constant evaluation of treatment goals and a continuous monitoring of the effects of treatment procedures on the client.

Behavioral counselors attempt to focus on what is objective, measurable, and amenable to replication (Franks and Brady, 1970). If hypothetical constructs such as consciousness, learning, self-awareness, or motivation are used, they are usually defined operationally (what people are *doing*) within a relatively rigorous behavioral and biological frame of reference. As Kanfer and Phillips (1970, p. 51) pointed out, this emphasis on observable events does not deny "the importance of behaviors that may not be accessible to observation at a given moment; nor does it reject the utility of a person's self-descriptions or verbal narratives about events." However, the use of hypothetical constructs without an accompanying operational definition may result in ambiguous descriptions and explanations.

Behavioral counseling is *not* confined to one discipline, to one school of thought, or to one S-R (stimulus-response) theory of learning (Franks and Brady, 1970). Behavioral counseling is multidimensional, utilizing procedures and strategies that are derived from a variety of learning principles. As Kanfer and Phillips (1970, p. 13) suggested, behavioral approaches for helping people require a repertoire of techniques for applying ". . . a unique combination of procedures (techniques) to fit individual cases." While generalized strategies have been developed and applied in behavioral counseling, the effects of these strategies must be uniquely determined and assessed for each client, group, institution, or environmental setting. The possible variations in resulting client consequences suggest considerable behavioral heterogeneity in the application and assessment of any particular procedure.

London (1972) declared that the distinguishing features of behavior therapy include the functional analysis of behavior and the development of the necessary technology to bring about change. Thus behavioral counseling is the application of specified procedures derived from experimental research to benefit an individual, a group, an institution, or an environmental setting. To facilitate the reader's understanding of the principles and procedures presented in the remaining chapters, three types of learning and several evaluation procedures are discussed.

Three Types of Learning

Hilgard and Bower defined learning as

> ... the process by which an activity originates or is changed through reacting to an encountered situation, provided that the characteristics of the change in activity cannot be explained on the basis of native response tendencies, maturation, or temporary states of the organism (e.g., fatigue, drugs, etc.) [Hilgard and Bower, 1966, p. 2].

Changing behavior can occur by any one or combination of the following three types of learning.

Operant (Instrumental) Learning (Conditioning)

Operant learning occurs when a neutral event or stimulus precedes a response or behavior and is followed by a negative, positive, or neutral consequence. For example, a child might be in a math class and be praised by the teacher for an oral recitation. The consequence of praising the child, depending on the child, could be negative (punishing — feels embarrassed), positive (rewarding — feels happy or proud), or neutral (feels neither happy nor bad). The specific consequence for the child could weaken the oral recitation (negative), strengthen it (positive), or have no effect at all (neutral).

In summary, an individual's response can be strengthened by reinforcement, or positive consequences, weakened by punishment or negative consequences, and extinguished by the absence of consequences. Figure 1 illustrates this learning process.

Notions of learning by consequences (i.e. reinforcement and punishment) have created fear that those who control and dispense the contingencies of reinforcement may be able to manipulate persons without knowledge and/or consent. Bandura has summarized the issue in stating:

Explanations of reinforcement originally assumed that consequences increase behavior without conscious involvement . . . although the empirical issue is not yet completely resolved, there is little evidence that rewards function as automatic strengtheners of human conduct. Behavior is not much affected by its consequences without awareness of what is being reinforced [1974, p. 860].

FIGURE 1

Diagram of the process of operant conditioning

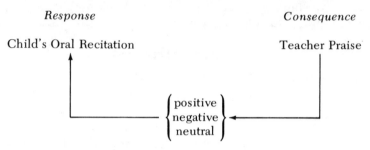

Response   *Consequence*

Child's Oral Recitation   Teacher Praise

Classical (Respondent) Conditioning (Learning)

The second type of learning is called classical conditioning or respondent learning. This type of learning involves the pairing (occurring in temporal contiguity) of a neutral event or stimulus with a stimulus that already elicits a reflexive response. For example, suppose a loud, boisterous voice from an adult elicits fear and anxiety from a child. The stimulus of a boisterous adult is called the unconditioned stimulus (UCS) because it already elicits a fear response (unconditioned response or UCR) from the child. A neutral stimulus could be, for our hypothetical example, a math class. If math class is paired with a boisterous teacher, after a time the math class alone could eventually elicit a fear response from the child. In Figure 2, the relationship of these stimuli in classical learning is diagrammed. Notice that after the pairing of the UCS and CS the math class alone can elicit the fear response. When this occurs, the fear response is labeled the conditioned response (CR) because a *new* stimulus condition (math class) has been conditioned to the fear response.

Bandura (1974) has challenged the popular belief that reflexive conditioning, or the pairing of two events in temporal proximity, is primarily responsible for the way humans learn.

People do not learn despite repetitive paired experiences unless they recognize that events are correlated. . . . The critical factor, therefore, is not that events occur together in time, but that people learn to predict them and to summon up appropriate anticipatory reactions. . . . The capacity to learn from correlated experiences reflects sensitivity, but because Pavlov first demonstrated the phenomenon with a dog, it has come to be regarded as a base animalistic process. . . . To expect people to remain unaffected by events that are frightening, humiliating, disgusting, sad, or pleasurable is to require that they be less than human [p. 859].

Some classical conditioning is said to be involved in the acquisition of a variety of behaviors such as attitudes, autonomic responses, fear, sexual behaviors, and to a great extent is involved in the desensitization or counterconditioning procedures discussed in Chapter 3. In using classical conditioning procedures, the counselor attempts to reduce, eliminate, or rearrange the conditioned response patterns. The technique or procedure is designed to change the stimulus control or cueing value of the antecedent stimulus (or stimuli). In contrast, the behavioral counselor employing operant or instrumental procedures of learning attempts to change the consequences of the environment instead of restructuring the stimuli pattern. Operant conditioning or learning focuses on active or voluntary responses and their consequences, while classical conditioning procedures involve a rearrangement of reflexive or involuntary response patterns to stimuli. How people learn or change their behavior is a complicated process and some have questioned the distinction between these two types of conditioning. However, operant and classical conditioning are helpful in assisting the behavior counselor in conceptualizing and designing therapeutic strategies and procedures.

FIGURE 2

Diagram of the process of classical conditioning

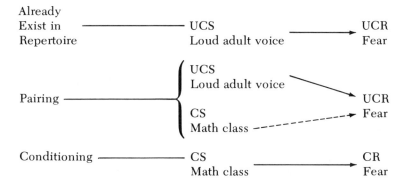

Social Modeling or Imitative Learning

Social modeling may be described as observational or imitative learning. Observational learning can result in the acquisition of new responses and in the strengthening or weakening of previously learned responses. Learning takes place through observation (and sometimes subsequent guided practice) of a model, presented in either live demonstration or symbolic (written manuals, films, video tapes, audio tapes) form. There are many factors associated with the effectiveness of imitative learning, including the characteristics of the model and the resulting consequences delivered to the model and/or the observer (i.e. client). In an excellent description of the role of social modeling in behavior acquisition, Bandura has stated:

> The capacity to represent modeled activities symbolically enables man to acquire new patterns of behavior observationally without reinforced enactment. From observing others one forms an idea of how certain behavior is performed and on later occasions the coded information serves as a guide for action. Indeed, research conducted within the framework of social learning theory shows that virtually all learning phenomena resulting from direct experience can occur on a vicarious basis by observing other people's behavior and its consequences for them . . . [1974, pp. 863–864].

Applications of social modeling in behavioral counseling will be discussed in Chapter 3.

Concepts of Behavioral Counseling

Antecedents and Consequences of Behavior

A helpful conceptual description for understanding the controlling conditions of behavior has been formulated (Thoresen, 1972; Mahoney and Thoresen, 1974). The behavior occurs between two environmental events or influences: antecedents (those that occur before or precede the behavior) and consequences (those that follow or occur after the behavior). Antecedent events can act as cues or stimulus controls for a specific behavior. For example, antecedents can be road signs or channel markers that are cues to inform you of probable consequences if you behave in a certain way. Consequences for behavior fall into three categories: positive, negative, and neutral. Consequences of a specific behavior will be idiosyncratic and will vary with each individual. For example, going out to dinner frequently may be positive for some people but eating out frequently may be negative for others. "ABCs" can apply to classical and to operant learning. Figure 3 illustrates the ABCs applied to our examples of operant and classical conditioning.

Shaping, Generalization, Discrimination, and Extinction

There are several principles or concepts that are frequently used in the jargon of behavioral counseling and can apply to all three types of learning. A brief discussion of these principles may facilitate a greater understanding of the strategies and procedures presented in the remaining chapters. *Shaping* or successive approximations means reinforcing responses that are successively closer to the desired response or behavior. For example, an adult may be successively reinforced for gradually eliminating the number of cigarettes smoked daily over a two week period, at which time no cigarettes are smoked. Also, the rate at which reinforcement is administered can have many different patterns. These patterns are called schedules of reinforcement. Fixed ratio or interval schedules have been demonstrated to be effective during the acquisition or initial stages of learning, while a variable ratio or interval schedule might be better in maintaining the learned behavior. As an illustra-

FIGURE 3

Diagram showing the antecedents, behavior, and consequences of an environmental event for classical and operant conditioning

	Antecedents (A)	*Behavior* (B)	*Consequences* (C)
	Boisterous Adult	Anxiety	Boisterous adult elicits anxiety reflexively
	Math class	No response	Math class is neutral
Classical Conditioning	Boisterous adult paired with Math class	Anxiety No response	Boisterous adult becomes associated with Math class
	Math class	Anxiety	Math class becomes a CS that elicits anxiety
Operant Conditioning	Teacher Question	Child's Oral Recitation	Teacher Praise: Positive Negative Neutral

tion, the schedules of reinforcement would be used in varying ways to increase the frequency of questions asked by a child in a classroom. Initially, the teacher would praise (potentially reinforce) the child for *every* question asked (fixed schedule), and later, teacher praise would follow a random or variable schedule; that is, some questions, but not every one, would be followed by teacher praise.

Generalization and discrimination are important concepts in behavioral counseling. When an individual responds similarly to several different situations or events, *generalization* has occurred. For example, a counselor who uses the same strategy or procedure for all clients who present different problems is an illustration of generalization. A complementary process to generalization is discrimination. In our above example, *discrimination* would occur when the counselor identifies different strategies or procedures which might be therapeutically beneficial for clients presenting specific problems. Also, discrimination training involves helping clients to identify (discriminate) different environmental cues or stimulus control conditions that might contribute to undesired behavior. Discrimination training would involve identifying the stimulus controlling environmental events and then changing the particular behavior pattern of responding to these events.

Extinction is a procedure for reducing or eliminating a behavior. In this procedure, the behavioral counselor determines what reinforcers are maintaining a problem behavior and attempts to remove or reorganize these reinforcers in order to eliminate the undesired behaviors. While reinforcers are removed or rearranged for the problem behavior, the counselor can simultaneously strengthen incompatible responses either by pairing or by reinforcing other more desirable responses.

Evaluation Procedures in Behavioral Counseling

Behavioral counseling includes the experimental investigation (including case study) and the systematic monitoring of the effects of treatment procedures on various client populations. The assessment of the effectiveness of counseling procedures is an extremely important process for the behavioral counselor. Franks and Wilson (1973, p. 5) have recommended that the important and appropriate question for people who use behavioral approaches for the treatment of human problems is "what *technique* should be applied to what *problem* in which *patient* by what therapist." Evaluation or research procedures used by behaviorists have ". . . begun to provide answers in the form of well-controlled studies comparing specific techniques with appropriate control conditions in the treatment of specific problem behaviors."

Behavioral scientists have developed and enhanced the research methodology employed by behavioral counselors, particularly with respect to single subject comparisons. In these studies, repeated observations (continuous monitoring) are made of one subject, one group of subjects, or one social unit over a period of time. Sidman (1960) pointed out the potential scientific rigor of the single subject designs, since a client (or a group or a social unit) can serve as his or her own control by comparing a series of observations of his or her behavior. Since behavioral counselors view all behavior as idiosyncratic and unique to each individual, the single subject designs may be particularly useful since the effects of a single application of a specific treatment can be assessed for each client. The single subject evaluation procedures are based on the time-series research designs described by Campbell and Stanley (1966) and more extensively by Glass, Willson, and Gottman (1972). There are four variations of single subject or time-series designs often used by behavioral counselors. These time-series variations will be discussed in greater detail than other evaluation procedures because they are referred to in some of the related research presented in the remainder of this monograph. Also, these particular time-series designs can be especially helpful for the behavioral counselor to use in monitoring the effects of a specific counseling strategy.

Time-Series Research Designs

In the first variation, little or no monitoring of the client's behavior occurs before a counseling procedure is introduced. In this variation, assessment of the client's behavior occurs only during and after a treatment has been implemented. This variation provides more limited evidence about the effects of a specific counseling procedure because fewer observations are made of the client's behavior before the counseling procedure is applied. However, this time-series variation may be the only evaluation procedure that can be used when it is inappropriate or impossible to obtain a lengthy baseline (pre-treatment) assessment. For example, after an initial interview with a client who reports a very high anxiety level at work, the counselor may decide that it is imperative for a counseling procedure, such as systematic desensitization, to be implemented immediately. As illustrated in Figure 4, only a brief baseline of one session (the in-take interview) on the client's anxiety level was obtained. Most of the observations were made during and after desensitization had been introduced (sessions 2–10).

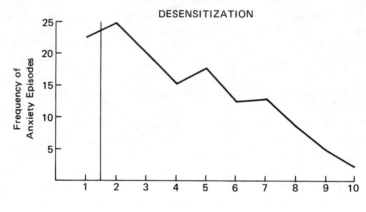

FIGURE 4

**Hypothetical results of after treatment only
single subject design**

DESENSITIZATION

Number of Counseling Sessions

The second time-series design, referred to as before-and-after treatment, involves fairly extensive monitoring of the client's behavior both before and after a particular counseling procedure is applied. This time-series variation is identical to the first one presented with the exception of a more lengthy baseline (i.e., monitoring before a counseling procedure). A hypothetical example of the before-and-after treatment time-series variation is presented in Figure 5. In this example, a Director of Pupil Personnel Services questioned the degree to which her staff in a particular school was involved in implementing aspects of a career education program as specified in a written policy statement at the beginning of the school year. The Director thought that the policy statement might be ambiguous. To ascertain the extent to which components of the career education program were being implemented, she conducted a three-month baseline on the number of completed components of the career education program. As illustrated in Figure 5, the treatment procedure, establishing specific objectives for the career education program, was introduced after the baseline, followed by further monitoring of the number of completed components (months 4–8) which increased after program objectives were established.

The third type of time-series variation involves obtaining a baseline before a treatment procedure, introducing a treatment

FIGURE 5

**Results of hypothetical study using before and after treatment
single subject design**

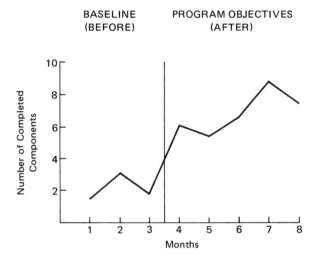

procedure followed by withdrawal or termination of treatment, after which a second baseline or no treatment period occurs. A hypothetical example is presented in Figure 6, in which a teacher used this design to assess the effects of a behavior contract on the number of books read by a student in his class. As depicted in Figure 6, the teacher monitored the number of books read in class for two months before the contract was introduced. The contract was in effect for two months. After this time, the contract terms were terminated and the number of books read was assessed for two months in a second baseline or no treatment period. A popular alternative to this design is to add a second treatment period after the second baseline. In our hypothetical example, a second contract treatment period could be added after Baseline 2. This time-series variation may not be appropriate to use in instances where it would be unethical to withdraw or terminate treatment (e.g., self-injurious behavior), or when the behavior under treatment is irreversible (e.g., reading comprehension).

When it is inappropriate to withdraw treatment, the behavioral counselor may use the last time-series variation, the multiple baseline designs. These designs can be used with one client to evaluate three or more different behaviors or to assess at least three different situations. In another application of this variation, multiple baseline designs can be used to evaluate the same variable for

FIGURE 6

Example of a single subject design with a second baseline

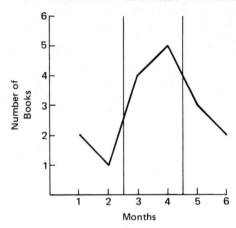

three different clients, groups, or social units. In a hypothetical example shown in Figure 7, a multiple baseline design was applied to three different rehabilitation centers to assess the effects of a vocational internship program on subsequent job placement of disabled clients. For the rehabilitation agency A, a baseline was conducted for three months, after which the internship program was introduced. Monitoring of the number of job placements continued for the remaining nine months. A longer baseline period occurred for agency B (the first six months) and an even more extensive baseline of nine months was conducted for agency C. Note that the internship program (i.e., treatment procedure) was staggered at different points in time for each of the three agencies. Applying the same treatment procedure for three or more situations at different times provides a way of comparing the effectiveness of one counseling or intervention strategy among several different settings or client populations. A particular counseling procedure, such as an internship program, can be considered effective if a change occurs in the dependent variable (e.g., job placements) at each point at which the treatment is introduced.

Some of the research studies described throughout these monographs have used the single subject or time-series designs to assess the treatment effects upon individual clients or settings. These designs are also referred to as idiographic, since observations for a single subject (i.e. client) or case are compared with the before treatment conditions if baseline data are collected. Other research studies illustrated have used a nomothetic or group comparison approach. In these research designs, the effects of a specified counseling procedure on a group of subjects are compared to a group who did not receive any treatment (control group) and/or to a group

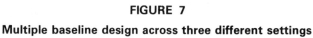

FIGURE 7

Multiple baseline design across three different settings

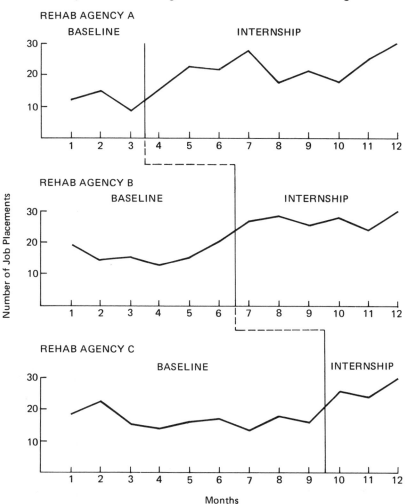

of subjects who received a variation of the treatment procedure. A large number of research studies are reported in the following chapters. The reader should be aware that the results of some of these studies may be influenced by methodology or research design as well as treatment procedures. For a more extensive discussion of research designs applicable to the behavioral counselor, the reader is referred to *Reading Statistics and Research* (Huck, Cormier, and Bounds, 1974).

Evaluation of treatment effects, either for the assessment of client progress, for research purposes, or both, is an important aspect of behavioral counseling. The role of evaluation conducted by behavioral counselors has been misunderstood by some to imply that a mechanistic application of evaluation procedures occurs. However, as Franks and Brady (1970) indicated:

> . . . the effective behavior therapist must be both a competent experimentalist and a sensitive, warm, human being, a person with a positive set of values and a firm belief in the dignity and worth of man, a humanist in the traditional sense in which this term was first used [p. 2].

No matter how rigorously a strategy has been investigated or how strongly a cause and effect relationship has been established, the effectiveness of the procedure will depend upon the client who uses the strategy and on the counselor who implements the procedure.

Historical Antecedents of Behavioral Counseling

One of the first contributors to the development of behavioral counseling was the Russian, Ivan Pavlov. In the latter part of his career, Pavlov (1927, 1941) recognized the possibility of applying classical or respondent conditioning techniques to psychotherapy. Pavlov explored the possibility of treating psychosis and neurosis with classical conditioning techniques. Earlier, in the United States, Watson and Rayner (1920) had conditioned a child to react with fear to a white rat and suggested that conditioning might be used as a therapeutic procedure to overcome certain neuroses. One of Watson's colleagues later demonstrated that the principles of conditioning could be applied to eliminate fears in children (Jones, 1924a; 1924b). The important contribution of applying learning theory to Freudian theory was made by Dollard and Miller in their book *Personality and Psychotherapy* (1950) and by Shoben (1949) in a paper entitled "Psychotherapy as a Problem in Learning Theory." Salter's *Conditioned Reflex Therapy* (1949) also aroused interest in the application of conditioning methods to abnormal behavior. The term "behavior therapy" is credited to Lindsley and Skinner who, in 1953, conducted research with the U.S. Navy Office of Naval Research, to determine the effects of operant conditioning techniques on the behavior of psychotic patients (Lazarus, 1971). A real impetus for behavior therapy was provided by the appearance of Lindsley's paper (1956) on the application of operant conditioning techniques to chronic schizophrenia. Wolpe's *Psychotherapy by Reciprocal Inhibition* (1958) was a major source for the development and introduction of a number of behavioral methods, particularly systematic desensitization. Another South African, Arnold Lazarus, argued for the need to add experimentally-derived therapeutic tools to psychotherapy (1958). In 1960, Eysenck edited an anthology of behavioral approaches to the treatment of neuroses, which provided further evidence for the techniques described by Wolpe and Lazarus. Bandura (1961), in his article entitled "Psychotherapy as a Learning Process," illustrated a variety of behavioral techniques such as positive reinforcement, counterconditioning, and modeling, and suggested that these approaches were not limited to external behaviors but could potentially be applied to covert responses as well. Krumboltz offered a behavioral approach to counseling in his *Revolution in Counseling* (1966b). In the same year, Thoresen (1966) presented an introduction of behavioral counseling for school counselors. In 1969, Krumboltz and Thoresen edited a published compendium of cases and techniques of behavioral counseling applied to educational settings. Hosford (1969b) presented an overview of behavioral counseling. Franks and Wilson (1973) have aptly summarized a historical perspective of behavioral counseling and therapy:

> An historian looking back on the brief history of behavior therapy might reasonably characterize the sixties as an era of expansion of the traditional S-R learning model into new settings. By the same token, if this first year is indicative of the coming trend, behavior therapy in the seventies *might* well be characterized by a further extension to encompass those areas of change seminal to our contemporary society: e.g. social movements, underprivileged groups, and political insitutions [p. 637].

There are many other persons who have assisted in the development of behavioral approaches for counseling. The contributions of most of these individuals have appeared in behavioral journals that have emerged within the last fifteen years: *Behaviour Research and Therapy* (1963), *Behavior Therapy and Experimental Psychiatry* (1970), *Journal of Applied Behavior Analysis* (1968), and *Behavior Therapy* (1970). Most of the case studies and the experimental evidence referred to in the following chapters have been selected from these journals. For a partial list of publications that report specific applications of behavioral procedures, see the Appendix.

In the remaining chapters, we have attempted to provide the reader with a sample of research (including case studies) illustrating the procedures associated with the principles of behavioral counseling. Chapter 2 presents initial procedures in behavioral counseling. Strategies associated with social modeling and classical learning are described in Chapter 3.

2

Initial Procedures in Behavioral Counseling

There are several prerequisites for the selection and implementation of behavioral counseling procedures. Applying a particular counseling procedure may be premature until certain preliminary procedures have been conducted. This chapter describes those initial procedures that cannot be excluded from the total behavioral counseling process. These include the application of *specific* verbal and nonverbal counselor behaviors that contribute to rapport, an accurate identification of the problem, and the establishment of counseling goals.

Verbal and Nonverbal Counselor Behavior

Historically, the counseling interaction has been described with vague and hypothetical constructs. Effective counseling has frequently been defined by such terms as "rapport," "empathy," and "unconditional positive regard." The use of these and similar terms, however, does not specify precisely what the counselor *does* to create rapport, to communicate empathy, or to convey unconditional positive regard. While behavioral counseling does not minimize the importance of rapport and empathy in therapeutic relationships, unless these terms are defined it is difficult to identify what the counselor can do to create and maintain an effective counseling interaction. Such concepts as empathy and rapport can be partially defined by specific verbal and nonverbal counselor behaviors. Throughout the history of counseling, verbal behavior has been viewed as the primary datum of the counseling interaction (Holz and Azrin, 1966; Loeffler, 1970). Recent emphasis has been placed on the importance of nonverbal behavior in the counseling interaction. A variety of experimental and descriptive research studies have yielded pertinent information that can be used to describe the counseling process in terms of both verbal and nonverbal behaviors (Zimmer and Anderson, 1968; Hackney, 1970). The behavioral counselor can employ these behaviors to create a facilitative atmosphere for client discussion of problems and goals.

Verbal Behavior

Research has provided some evidence to indicate that a systematic relationship exists between the verbal behavior of the counselor and the client's responses. This relationship has been demonstrated in several classic studies (Greenspoon, 1955; Verplanck, 1955; and Azrin, Holz, Ulrich, and Goldiamond, 1961). These studies showed that the experimenter's verbal behavior had a systematic influence on the subsequent behavior of the subjects, who either increased or decreased a particular behavior following verbal reinforcement or extinction by the experimenter.

More recently, similar studies have investigated the effects of verbal behaviors in quasi-counseling settings. Modifications in client verbal behavior have occurred as a direct result of the counselor's or the experimenter's selective use of specific verbal responses, including minimal verbal stimuli, reflection, and paraphrase (Rogers, 1960; Salzinger, 1960; Waskow, 1962; Merbaum, 1963; Kennedy and Zimmer. 1968: Pepyne, 1968; Crowley, 1970; and Auerswald, 1974). Pepyne and Zimmer (1969) have concluded that specific changes in a client's verbal behavior may be predicted and explained.

Recent investigations of the influence of the counselor's verbal behavior on the client have attempted to discover the specific types of counselor verbal behaviors that occur within the counseling interaction. Factor analysis of counselor-client communications has revealed that a finite number of verbal responses exist within a counselor's repertoire (Zimmer and Park, 1967; Zimmer, Wightman, and McArthur, 1970; Zimmer and Pepyne, 1971; Tilley, 1972). The result of their pioneering studies is a list and description of thirty-one verbal responses, as presented in Table 1 (Zimmer and Pepyne, 1971). The information provided by these studies enables the counseling process to be defined, to a large extent, in an operational manner. It is now possible to describe precisely the types of verbal responses emitted by the counselor in a typical counseling interaction. Defining verbal behaviors operationally allows counselor education programs to train counselors in specific behaviors and skills instead of generalized constructs. The success of training counselors may be an artifact of the extent to which the counseling techniques have been operationally defined.

TABLE 1

Counselor Verbal Responses

1. *Information giving* — a statement which conveys objective data or information, as opposed to subjective opinion.
2. *Formal explication* — a formal, pedantic examination of the general nature of the client's difficulty, a logical analysis of corrective measures.
3. *Establishing cognitive set* — counselor proceeds to use an abstract third person as a referent.
4. *Clarification of cause and effect* — characterized by labeling and identification of cause and effect relationships.
5. *Interpretation* — the counselor transforms the client's statements by using data selectively and the interpretation is characterized by ambiguous referents.
6. *Accenting* — restatement of a single word or phrase from a previous client response.
7. *Role definition* — characterized by establishing the counselor as an expert.
8. *Command* — the counselor orders or directs the client's behavior.

9. *Urging assertive reaction* — the client is prodded or urged toward an explicit reaction to the counselor or setting.
10. *Process potential* — the counselor points out and refers to the client's current potential for entering into a defined activity.
11. *Eliciting assertive verbal behavior* — the counselor tells the client what to say. Elicited statements take the form of an attack on the counselor.
12. *Ability potential* — supportive type responses suggesting behaviors or achievements the client could or could not manifest.
13. *Confrontation* — the counselor reflects a communication emitted by the client but follows it by specifying an apparent contradictory communication or behavior.
14. *Clarification by antagonistically toned statements* — the counselor jolts the client from a presumptive line of thought through a denial of the client's statement.

TABLE 1

Counselor Verbal Responses (continued)

15. *Identifying incongruities* —reference is made to conflicting cues being emitted by the client.
16. *Badgering* — the counselor repeats his own words, phrases, or statements.
17. *Counselor-directed shift of approach* — the counselor intentionally shifts either the topic under discussion or the course of the interview.
18. *Eliciting ambiguity* — the counselor's statement contains ambivalent constructions.
19. *Modeling* — the counselor reveals his own subjective, cognitive, or affective processes for the purpose of demonstrating responses.
20. *Establish affect set* — an introduction and invitation to talk with references to affect and relationships.
21. *Unstructured invitation* — counselor leads which elicit verbal responses but do not specify or limit the content or mood.
22. *Summarization* — paraphrases which condense the semantic content or identify the common theme of several client responses.
23. *Relativistic measures* — a "yardstick" or standard is used by the counselor as a direct perspective for the particular client problem.
24. *Clarification of role conflict* — a statement that points out the relationship between the client and a third person and primarily emphasizes the client's "feelings."
25. *Establishing connections* — selective restatements of multiple elements of the client's verbal and nonverbal communications.
26. *Restatement* — repeating client responses typically substituting "you" for "I" or stating condensed abridgements.
27. *Reflection* — statements of observations of client nonverbal behavior of paraphrasing selected components of the client's verbal responses.
28. *Probes* — interrogative responses which require a procedural reply rather than a single "yes" or "no."
29. *Rhetorical question* — a statement verbalized as a question asked solely to produce an effect or make an assertion.
30. *Minimal social stimulus* — vocalizations such as "mm-hm," "oh," "good," etc., or nonverbal stimuli such as head nods, smiles, etc.
31. *Recognition of value in ambiguous client statement* — explicit approval by the counselor when the client is unable to fully verbalize his thinking.

Nonverbal Behavior

Similar studies have attempted to define more precisely the types of nonverbal counselor behaviors and ther subsequent effects on client behavior. A factor analysis of the movements of seventeen pairs of counselor-client dyads (Fretz, 1966) yielded ten distinct nonverbal counselor behaviors (Table 2). Further specificity of the effects of postural and gestural nonverbal interviewer behaviors on conveying affiliative attitudes (conjunctive behavior) or less affiliative attitudes (disjunctive behaviors) to interviewees was provided by Smith (1972). Forward trunk lean, gesturing, positive nods, smiles and laughs, and quasi-courtship behaviors (preening) communicated affiliative attitudes. Changes in trunk position, a side trunk position, negative nods, looking away, leg and foot movements, and lip and tongue movements conveyed a less affiliative attitude. In a study investigating the components of empathy, Haase and Tepper (1972) found that two nonverbal behaviors, forward trunk lean and direct eye contact, accounted for twice the variability as the verbal element of the empathic message, suggesting that empathy may be conveyed more by nonverbal than verbal counselor behaviors.

Specific effects of certain nonverbal behaviors have been investigated in a variety of studies. Eye contact was found to be an important variable in communicating attention (Ivey, 1971) and also in raising the level of perceived empathy when used in conjunction with a verbal empathic message (Haase and Tepper, 1972). In investigating the effects of distance in dyadic settings, Haase (1970) found that students viewed a closer interaction distance (30 and 39 inches) as most appropriate for counselor interactions. Haase and Tepper's study (1972) revealed that a close interaction distance (32 inches) raised the perceived level of empathy in a counseling interview, while a far interaction distance (72 inches) significantly lowered the judged level of communicated empathy. In studying counselor-client interactions, Fretz (1966) found that gestures, in the form of hand movements, were the best indicators of satisfaction as reported by both clients and counselors. Similar findings were reported by Smith (1972). The studies conducted by Fretz and Smith also revealed that highly favorable counseling and social relationships were characterized by more positive head nods and fewer negative head nods. Perception of a positive dyadic relationship also appears to be correlated with a forward trunk lean and with a body orientation directly facing the client (Fretz, 1966; Smith, 1972).

TABLE 2

Nonverbal Counselor Behaviors

Nonverbal Behaviors	Clients	Counselors
1) Horizontal Hand Movements	Both Hands Out Both Hands Circle Right Hand Out Right Hand to Knee Right Hand Circles Left Hand Out Left Hand Circles	Both Hands Out Right Hand Out Right Hand to Knee
2) Vertical Hand Movements	 Right Hand to Chin Right Hand Up & Down Left Hand Up & Down	Both Hands Clasp at Chin Right Hand Up & Down Left Hand Up & Down
3) Head Movements Other than Nods	Head Erect Head Forward Head Back Head Turn Left Head Turn Right Head Tilts	Head Erect Head Forward Head Back Head Turn Left Head Turn Right
4) Positive Nod		Positive Nod
5) Negative Nod/ Points	Negative Nod/ Points	Negative Nod
6) Smile and Laugh	Smile Laugh	Smile Laugh
7) Lead Forward, Lean Back		Lean Forward Lean Back
8) "Talk-Stop"	Right Hand to Lap Left Hand to Lap Chin Leans on Hand	
9) "Thinking"	Looks Up Eyebrows Raised	Looks Up Eyebrows Raised
10) Clasping Movements	Both Hands Clasp Both Hands Clasp at Lap Finger Play Plays with Something	

From B. R. Fretz. Postural movements in a counseling dyad. *Journal of Counseling Psychology*, 1966, *13*, 335–343. Copyright 1966 by the American Psychological Association.

Effects of Counselor Behaviors

The results of these studies permit counselors to identify the variety of verbal and nonverbal responses in their behavioral repertoire. Becoming aware of verbal and nonverbal behaviors demonstrated in the interaction may permit the counselor to identify the effects of these behaviors on subsequent client responses (Cormier and Nye, 1973). Two recent research studies support the notion that counselor behavior produces differential rather than generalizable responses from individual clients. Hackstian, Zimmer, and Newby (1971) have shown that the same client responded differently when in client-centered therapy, rational-emotive therapy, and gestalt therapy on seven out of seven dependent variables. Barnabei, Cormier, and Nye (1974) found that three counselor responses — reflection of feeling, probe, and confrontation — do not necessarily yield such predicted client responses as self referent statements, self-exploration, and a greater amount of verbal affect. It may be concluded that behavioral counseling cannot, like other theoretical orientations in counseling, be described as a predetermined and stylized activity (Thoresen and Hosford, 1973). Instead, behavioral counseling may be viewed as a "functional relationship between the counselor's behavior and subsequent client responses [Cormier and Nye, 1973, p. 2]." The basic counselor function involved in behavioral counseling is defined as discrimination; that is, the differential responding to different situations (individuals, groups, institutions, and environmental settings). Discrimination, as used in behavioral counseling approaches, suggests that the counselor has acquired some discriminative capacities about his or her own overt and covert behaviors (self development), can identify the types of procedures used in counseling (repertoire development) and, most importantly, can discriminate the effects of these procedures on resulting client consequences (process development) (Cormier and Nye, 1973). In behavioral counseling, the effectiveness of the counselor is determined by continuous assessments of the effects of each counseling procedure upon resulting client outcomes, rather than upon predetermined theoretical biases and/or counseling styles.

Problem Identification

Two initial procedures in behavioral counseling involve identifying the client's problem and establishing counseling goals that reflect changes in behavior or problem solutions desired by the client. Communication is the mode by which problems are identified and goals are established. However, sometimes the language of communication between the counselor and client can become distorted. For example, a client may come in and state that he/she is depressed. The counselor's concept of depression may be radically different than the feelings and behaviors that the client intends to convey by that word. There is another problem that is often complicated by disparities in counselor-client communication modes. For example, a teacher or a parent may come to a counselor and request help with a "hyperactive" child. Communicating in this way assumes that the child is *generally* hyperactive and neglects to determine how hyperactivity is manifested (i.e., what does the child *do*) and *when* and *under what conditions* hyperactivity occurs. Communication also involves problem identification and goal setting with social institutions and organizations, as well as with individual clients and groups. For example, a counselor may be required to streamline certain institutional processes and/or procedures because of their dehumanizing effect(s) on the people that the institution is designed to serve. In such cases, the counselor must be able to determine the specific behaviors that contribute to the dehumanization in order to bring about necessary change.

Operational Definitions

In problem identification, one primary counselor function is to translate vague, ambiguous client concerns into specific observable behaviors. This translation process can be referred to as using "operational definitions." For example, the concept of learning may be defined by its outcome such as reducing the number of cigarettes smoked daily, decreasing negative self talk, swimming 50 yards, demonstrating so many appropriate job interview behaviors, or leading a structured activity within a group setting. In other words, the concept of learning is defined by the operations or outcomes of a process. When a concept or process such as learning is defined in this way, it can be objectively evaluated. Similarly, a client may report to a counselor that she/he has difficulty in getting along with other people. Unless this description is translated into an operational definition, the counselor may never determine exactly with what the client is concerned and in what ways the client would like to be different. For one client, "having difficulty in getting along with people" might mean not being able to say "no" to people and wanting to be more assertive, while for another client it may mean feeling uncomfortable in a large group of strangers and wanting to be more relaxed and talkative. Thus, an operational definition involves defining a hypothetical construct, such as learning or getting along with people, in terms of the specific behaviors associated with the process or with the individual. Operational definitions serve the following purposes in the process of problem identification:

1. Precise definitions can establish a clear understanding between the counselor and client regarding the identified problems and goals, helping to insure that the direction of counseling is agreed upon cooperatively and that client progress and change is assessed.
2. Precise definitions allow the client and counselor to determine *when* a particular behavior occurs, so that it is specifically rather than globally assessed.
3. Operational definitions can prevent the counselor from making inaccurate references about the client, projected from his/her own biases rather than from actual client data. Being able to define processes in operational terms requires recognition and identification of various behavior categories.

Overt and Covert Behavior Descriptions

Translating generalized statements of client concerns and feelings into specific behaviors is not always an easy process. For example, a counselor may label and infer that a client is "anxious" without being able to verify that description from actual observed client behaviors, that may include speech errors (stammers, repetitions), rapidity in rate of speech, tightly clasped hands, arms or legs, body indications of sweat, darting eyes or averted eye contact, twisting of an object, etc. These items are some examples of client nonverbal and paralanguage behavior identifications. However, a collection of behaviors such as the ones described in the above example may not necessarily connote anxiety. In some cases, a client who exhibits some or all of these behaviors may not be feeling well, may be tired, or may be experiencing back pains.

These examples describe two frequently used classifications of behavior: *overt* and *covert*. Overt behaviors may be divided into two categories: *verbal* and *nonverbal*. For example, verbal behaviors include all spoken words emitted by a client. Hackney and Nye (1973) have referred to verbal language as primarily *cognitive* (events, people, facts, things) or *affective* (feelings, emotions). Examples of nonverbal behaviors include paralinguistics (voice quality, tone, pitch, rate of speech), proxemics (body space, distance, territoriality), facial expression, body posture, and body movements. Nonverbal behavior also includes specific actions performed by a person, such as a sequence of activities performed by a surgeon, a variety of foot patterns exhibited by a ballerina, and the running and jumping of an active child. While verbal and nonverbal overt behaviors are *directly* observable (i.e., they can be clearly seen), covert processes can only be inferred or assumed. Covert behaviors include problem solving (cognition), feelings (emotions), memory, perceptions, axiological systems (values, attitudes, beliefs), symbolic processes, and physiological states. Covert behaviors are more remote and less accessible than overt behaviors. Any assumption made by the counselor regarding a client's covert process should be checked out directly with the client in order to verify the accuracy of the counselor's interpretation. For example, a group leader may think that a group member is "depressed" because of some overt behaviors displayed in the group session, such as lack of verbal participation, concerned facial expression (e.g., downcast eyes, dropped jaw), and stooped body position. In such a case, the group leader can use the member's observable data to check out his/her inference that the member is feeling "depressed" (covert behavior). Rather than saying "You are depressed," the leader can say "You look depressed since you aren't talking, have a serious look on your face, and are sitting in a slumped manner."

The problem of discriminating between an individual's overt and covert behavior also confronts the counselor in consulting with teachers and parents. Usually a teacher or a parent describes the child in a manner that makes an inference about the child's covert processes: "This child is disruptive" or "I have a naughty boy" or "What can I do about my withdrawn child?" (Institutions engage in the same behavior by labeling an individual as autistic, schizophrenic, etc.) The counselor's task is to assist the teacher, parent, or client in identifying a pattern of observable behaviors. Problem identification in behavioral counseling seeks to assess the response capability of the client rather than to classify client problems based on a diagnostic system (Thoresen and Hosford, 1973).

Information Gathering

There are generally three procedures for gathering information about a client's problem behavior(s). Any one procedure, or any combination of the three, or all three collectively, can be used with a client. The first procedure involves systematic observational techniques that can be used to observe a client in naturalistic settings. The second procedure consists of schedules and checklists for assessing client problems. The last procedure is the one perhaps most typically used by behavioral counselors. The counselor, usually in conjunction with the client, designs a method for assessing the client's problem behavior and providing a functional analysis of environmental events.

Systematic Observational Procedures

Sometimes counselors have to teach others (parents, teachers, students, paraprofessionals) to map the behavior of a client. There are two commonly used techniques for observing and measuring behavior. With the first technique, the observer records the *frequency* of the behavior occurring within a specified time period. For example, a teacher might want to know how many math problems a student can solve correctly during a 50-minute class period or a client might want to record the number of times he/she feels anxious during the day. A second technique is to record the *duration or amount of time* a client engages in a particular behavior during a session or time period. For example, with a stop watch, an observer (or client) can record the cumulative amount of time a client engages in a behavior. The reliability of behavior observation is very important in the counseling process. Without a relatively high (usually above 85%) agreement about the behavior being observed, it is difficult for the counselor to define accurately the behavior being observed and to make recommendations about behavioral change. These observational techniques are similar to those described elsewhere in considerable detail by Bijou, Peterson, and Ault (1968) and Bijou, Peterson, Harris, Allen, and Johnston (1969). Observation also may be conducted by the client. A client can use a daily record sheet to record information about the problem including time of day, activities engaged in, and antecedent and consequent events.

Assessment Checklists

The second procedure used by behavioral counselors for assessing a client's problem involves the client's completion of one or several schedules or checklists. Background information on the client can be obtained by using the *Life History Questionnaire* (Wolpe and Lazarus, 1966). Several schedules have been developed for determining what events or things might be reinforcing to the client (Cautela and Kastenbaum, 1967), and for fears a client might have (Wolpe and Lang, 1964; Geer, 1965). A problem checklist for use in assessing family verbal behavior (Thomas, Walter, and O'Flaherty, 1974), a schedule for determining assertive behavior (Rathus, 1973a), a self-expression scale for measuring assertiveness of college students (Galassi, Delo, Galassi, and Bastien, 1974), and a checklist for pinpointing behavior in school, home, or community (Wahler and Cormier, 1970) are other examples of behavioral measurement tools that can be used in problem identification.

Behavior and Environmental Descriptions

The third procedure may combine some or all aspects of the above two procedures. Additionally, this procedure involves identifying the behavior and specific environmental events that are uniquely associated with the client's problem (Cormier and Cormier, 1974a). In obtaining a behavioral description of the problem, the counselor must select and implement those responses that encourage the client to focus on behaviors and actions. A client who reports feelings of depression needs to identify the actions and behaviors that contribute to such feelings. Some examples of counselor responses used to elicit behavioral descriptions are: "What do you mean by saying your life is empty now?" "Give me some specific instances of times when you feel like getting a divorce." "What are you doing when you're upset?"

The third procedure in identifying client problems and concerns also involves determining the conditions or circumstances that are associated with the problem. The counselor seeks to ascertain where and when the client is engaging in these actions or behaviors. Identifying conditions associated with the problem gives the counselor important data, since in some cases specific conditions contribute to the problem. The behavioral counselor can use this data to discriminate whether the conditions, the behavior, or both can be changed, and future counseling strategies can be planned accordingly.

Three types of conditions associated with a problem may be identified. One type, described above, involves the circumstances under which the problem occurs. A counselor might ask a client "When does this usually happen?" and "Where are you when this happens?" For some clients, identifying where and when the behavior occurs may be sufficient. With other clients, the counselor may have to obtain a description of two other types of related conditions, including the antecedents, those events that preceded the action, and the consequences, those events that followed the action. The counselor can use leads similar to the following to identify antecedent and consequent conditions: "What happens just before the fights?"; "What have you noticed you're doing or not doing just before these arguments?"; "What happens after the fights?"; or "What do you think goes on following the arguments?" This is an important description in cases where consistent conditions occur before and after the undesired behavior. As the reader will recall from the discussion in Chapter 1, identifying antecedent and consequent conditions is not always an easy process. The set of conditions that precede and that follow a problem may not always be in immediate temporal proximity to the identified problem. Also, the antecedent and consequent conditions may, in some cases, be covert as well as overt events.

One essential process of problem identification is for the counselor, with the help of the client, to make accurate discriminations about presenting client concerns. Based upon these discriminations, the counselor may choose to implement those strategies that could facilitate discussion of client behaviors and possible environmental conditions associated with the problem. Objective and accurate problem identification is the prerequisite for establishing the goals of counseling. With vague and inaccurate problem identification, goals may be established which are valid counseling goals, but inappropriate for the defined problem.

Establishing Goals

Following accurate assessment of the client's problem, and based on data accumulated within the problem identification process, goals are established by the counselor and client which reflect the client's expectations of counseling results in behavioral terms. Clients benefit by observable goals that specify what they expect from counseling. Goals identify the purpose of counseling and provide a basis for the counselor to plan, implement, and evaluate the particular use of a counseling strategy. Goals serve as bench marks that can provide continuous indications of client progress. Stating counseling goals explicitly minimizes the ambiguity of vague theoretical approaches or therapeutic outcomes (Cormier and Cormier, 1974b). Bandura (1969) has summarized the functions of well-defined objectives:

> Behaviorally defined objectives not only provide guidance in selecting appropriate procedures, but they serve an important evaluative function as well. When desired outcomes are designated in observable and measurable terms, it becomes readily apparent when the methods have succeeded, when they have failed, and when they need further development to increase their potency. This self-corrective feature is a safeguard against perpetuation of ineffective approaches, which are difficult to retire if the changes they are supposed to produce remain ambiguous [p. 74].

Counseling objectives may be classified according to *process* and *outcome* goals (Hackney and Nye, 1973). Although not mutually exclusive, *process* goals refer to the conditions of the relationship, while *outcome* goals specify the desired behavior change of the client. Process goals refer to the qualities of the relationship and level of participation between the client and counselor, or among the group members. For example, process goals may include reducing anxiety in the counseling setting, and eliciting verbal participation within the dyadic, group, or institutional setting. In contrast, outcome goals refer to the client's actions and behaviors demonstrated in the environment, as a consequence of individual counseling, a group experience, or a consultation intervention. Examples of possible outcome goals for individual clients may include losing a specified amount of weight, improving grades, and being assertive in social situations. Often group members may specify such outcome goals as talking positively about oneself, attending to interpersonal feedback, and spending more time with one's children. Institutional outcome goals may include reducing the number of forms to be completed by clientele, increasing the number of innovative services to clientele, establishing a relevant in-service training program for staff members, and defining procedures to evaluate the validity of services provided to clientele.

Outcome Goals: Behavior, Condition, Level

Outcome goals, in order to provide indications of progress and change, should contain three parts (Mager, 1962; Bandura, 1969). The first part specifies what the client is to *do*. In other words, this part defines the behaviors (overt and covert) that the client would like to demonstrate as a result of counseling. Specifying the goal in behavioral terms makes the results of counseling more apparent. The client and the counselor can use a behavioral index to observe how and when the desired behavior change occurs.

Specifying *the conditions* under which the behaviors are to occur is the second part of an outcome goal. For most clients, the identified problem behavior is elicited and maintained by a *particular* set of environmental circumstances or conditions that may include the responses of the client. For example, a client may report anxiety in large group situations but not in small groups. Or, a client may be able to be assertive with his/her supervisor, but not with his/her spouse.

The third part of an outcome goal includes the *level* or *extent* to which the client is to demonstrate the behavior. A client may report reduced smoking (behavior) at work (condition) during the previous week or since the last counseling session, but may not be sure about the actual number of cigarettes smoked daily while at work.

Unless a client can specify the extent to which he/she desires to change the behavior (e.g., smoking), the client and counselor will have difficulty in determing accurately whether the goal has been reached, and when. Some examples of specifying the extent or degree of the behavior to be increased or decreased by a client include reducing weight by five pounds each week, increasing achievement in a math class by one letter grade during a six week period, or increasing assertive behavior by initiating four social conversations a week.

Who Determines the Goals?

In most counseling settings, the client is primarily responsible for deciding upon the specific behaviors to be changed, based upon his/her expectations or reasons for seeking counseling. Establishing goals is, at best, a cooperative venture between the counselor and client. Since clients often present their expectations for counseling in a vague and ambiguous manner, the counselor is responsible for clarifying and defining the desired goals in behavioral terms and also for presenting alternative goals that may help the client to attain those expectations. In helping the client to establish outcome goals, the counselor must take care to avoid imposing goals that reflect his/her theoretical biases and could interfere with the client's desired objectives. If the counselor's own values are in strong conflict with the goals suggested by the client, referral to another counselor may be initiated (Krumboltz, 1966a; Bandura, 1969).

In determining behavioral goals with clients, the counselor should be aware of some specific problems that may prevent accurate definition of goals. Krumboltz and Thoresen (1969 pp. 9–18) listed seven potential stumbling blocks in establishing counseling goals:

1. The client views his problem as someone else's behavior.
2. The client expresses the problem as a *feeling*.
3. The problem is the absence of a goal.
4. The problem is that a desired behavior is undesirable.
5. The problem is that the client does not know his behavior is inappropriate.
6. The problem is a choice conflict.
7. The problem is a vested interest in not identifying any problem.

Steps in Establishing Goals

Cormier and Cormier (1974b) have summarized the steps in goal setting as follows:

1. *Discussing client expectations.* The counselor must ask the client how he/she would like to change his/her behavior. Although the client may allude to desired changes while discussing his/her problems, the counselor should initiate the process of goal setting by having the client specify exactly how she/he would like things to be different as a result of counseling. The type and direction of change desired by the client may dictate the counseling procedures used to help the client achieve his or her expectations.

2. *Obtaining client commitment.* Establishing client goals is more effective when the counselor has obtained a verbal commitment from the client to carry out specified procedures in order to achieve those goals. The counselor can do this by asking if the client is willing to make an effort both within and outside of the interview setting to complete the actions necessary for goal attainment. Client commitment verifies to the counselor that the client is serious about achieving goals. Occasionally, seeking to obtain a commitment may be valuable in another way, by indicating client hesitation or resistance to goal setting. When this occurs, the counselor should initiate a discussion about the apparent resistance.

3. *Establishing client goals.* The counselor and client together must agree upon the specific goals that the client desires to reach as a result of counseling. To do this, the counselor may need to assist the client in translating vague statements of concern into specific outcome goals. The counselor should allow the client to specify the goal; then the counselor should help the client to state the goal in observable, behavioral terms that specify what the client will be *doing* when the goal is reached. Additionally, the counselor should assist the client in identifying the *level* or extent to which he/she will be satisfied with change, and the *conditions* under which the client expects or desires the change to occur.

4. *Determining client alternatives.* After a specific goal has been identified, the counselor should help the client establish alternatives — ideas or actions that will enable the client to reach the goal in an effective manner. Usually, during problem identification, it becomes apparent that there are other more effective behaviors or solutions for the client than what he/she is presently doing. The counselor should ask the client to specify possible alternatives that may help to resolve the problem and/or make things different. If the counselor is aware of additional alternatives, these could be suggested for the client's consideration.

5. *Identifying sub-goals.* Often the goal that is specified by the client is an overall or ultimate goal that may take several months or longer to complete. It would be a difficult task for any client to

reach this goal without making small steps of progress along the way. Therefore, the counselor must help the client identify and engage in various sub-goals that represent "successive approximations." These sub-goals help the client to work on small behaviors one at a time so that the overall goal is achieved gradually and successfully.

As Bandura observed, "although the specification of ultimate objectives provides some direction and continuity to a program of change, day-to-day progress is most influenced by defining intermediate objectives and the learning experiences necessary for their attainment [1969, p. 74]." Bandura also noted that skillful sequencing of sub-goals can help in achieving desired objectives by reducing the likelihood of failure on successive sub-tasks, maintaining a high level of positive reinforcement through continuous progress, and allowing for quality control over learning or counseling outcomes.

6. *Establishing action steps.* Once a list of sub-goals has been identified, the counselor should help the client choose one sub-goal to work on prior to the next session "check-in" point; this way the client will attain the sub-goals gradually as counseling progresses. As each sub-goal is identified, it may become apparent that in order for the client to achieve that goal, one or more action steps will have to be taken. For example, if a client's overall goal is to be assertive with females, and a sub-goal involves asking two girls out for a date, the client will need to engage in the action steps of making two telephone calls or verbal requests. The counselor should help the client identify and select any action step necessary to complete the sub-goal. The action step might be rehearsed within the interview to insure the probability that the client will be successful in his/her attempts. The client should report his/her action steps to the counselor and should receive immediate support for successful completion.

Goal-setting in counseling is a dynamic process that involves flexibility and the opportunity to redefine the objectives originally identified by the client. The establishment of original goals should be tentative in order to provide opportunities for the client to try out new behaviors and to examine resulting consequences. In the course of this exploration phase, originally stated goals may change. Additionally, other problem areas may be defined in the course of counseling that reflect different objectives. Counseling interventions can be adapted for these new objectives with appropriate specification of new learning experiences. Commenting on the lack of irrevocability in the client's decision-making process, Bandura noted that "by retaining flexibility in the selection, sequencing, and timing of objectives, the treatment program remains highly sensitive to feedback from resultant changes [1969, p. 104]."

3

Strategies Based on Social Modeling and Classical Learning

A collection of procedures that can be applied either to an individual or to a group of clients is presented in this chapter. While various behavioral strategies are presented in separate sections, the reader will observe that areas of overlap exist among procedures. Social modeling, behavior rehearsal, and assertive training are used primarily to facilitate acquisition or strengthening of a behavior, while systematic desensitization, flooding, implosion, and aversive therapy are more typically applied to weaken or to eliminate an undesirable response. In actual practice, however, it is likely that two or more of these procedures may be used in conjunction to treat different components of the identified problem. The principles, related research, and suggested procedural considerations are presented for each strategy. Obviously, some of the procedures may be more applicable in schools, while others may be more easily adapted to a clinical setting. All strategies should be applied only when the counselor has a thorough command of the necessary procedures.

Social Modeling

One type of learning considered in Chapter 1 was social modeling. This powerful learning process has also been referred to as observational learning, copying, imitation, identification, vicarious learning, or social facilitation (Bandura, 1969). Social modeling is one of the processes by which children learn a complex sequence of behaviors. Through national media, friendships, social groups, and organizations, adults also acquire or learn a great deal of their different responses and patterns of behavior by this vicarious process. As a procedure in behavioral counseling, modeling is generally used to acquire new responses, to strengthen or weaken behaviors already in the client's repertoire, or to facilitate the occurrence of previously learned responses (Bandura and Walters, 1963; Bandura, 1965).

Social modeling can involve the presentation of live (physically present) or symbolic models (films, audio- or video-tapes, and written descriptions). Symbolic models may have effects similar to live models as long as the behaviors to be learned are clearly specified with sufficient details (Bandura and Mischel, 1965; Prentice, 1972). Usually the detailed specification of the behavior to be learned is presented in written instructions. Evidence suggests that modeling procedures combined with written instruction are most effective in observational learning (Whalen, 1969; Green and Marlatt, 1972). Bandura (1969) stated that instructions accompanying modeling are more likely to result in correct performance when they both activate a person to respond and describe the appropriate responses and the order in which those responses are to occur. Using live models to promote desired behaviors has been documented in a variety of experimental investigations (Bandura, Ross, and Ross, 1963; Ryan, 1965, 1966; Wallace, Davis, Liberman, and Baker, 1973). Successful presentation of symbolic models has involved the use of film models (Walters, Leat, and Mezei, 1963; O'Connor, 1969), video-taped models (Varenhorst, 1964; Myrick, 1969; Atkinson, 1971; Frankel, 1971; Smith and Lewis, 1974), audio-taped models (Kanfer and Marston, 1963; Wheeler and Caggiula, 1966; Green and Marlatt, 1972; Goldstein, Martens, Hubben, van Bell, Schaaf, Wiersma, and Goedhart, 1973), and written instructional manuals (LaFleur and Johnson, 1972).

The characteristics of the model are important factors contributing to the success of social modeling as a counseling procedure. Some of the most prominent characteristics that should be considered in selecting models include sex of the model (Schroeder, 1964; Thoresen, 1964; Thoresen, Krumboltz, and Varenhorst, 1965, 1967), prestige of the model (Krumboltz, Varenhorst, and Thoresen, 1967; Thoresen and Hamilton, 1972), athletic, social, and academic success of the model (Thoresen and Krumboltz, 1968; Thoresen and Hamilton, 1972), and ethnic background (Hosford and De-

Visser, 1972; Stilwell and Thoresen, 1972). More extensive evidence of the effects of these characteristics is presented by Hosford (1969b) and Mischel (1971).

Social modeling can be applied to a variety of settings and can be used with numerous other procedures. Modeling is an important element in most of the other behavioral procedures presented in this chapter. To this date, social modeling procedures have been used extensively in dyadic and group counseling with an increasing emphasis on preventive techniques in school, clinical, and community settings. Social modeling may be used more in the future as a training procedure for acquisition of such skills as decision-making, creative problem-solving, job interviewing, and communication.

Behavior Acquisition

The following studies reported the use of social modeling to acquire or strengthen behaviors in schools and in clinical settings. Krumboltz and his associates were among the first persons to apply social modeling procedures to school settings in a unique way (Krumboltz and Thoresen, 1964; Thoresen, 1964; Schroeder, 1964; Krumboltz and Schroeder, 1965). The first four studies reported by Krumboltz and his associates were all variations of the same experimental procedures in which two social modeling treatment procedures were compared. One treatment involved reinforcement counseling, in which the counselor reinforced (verbally and by gestures) desired client verbal statements. The other treatment used model-reinforcement counseling, in which the above procedure was included with the addition of two fifteen-minute audio-taped models. The audio-tapes were models of a brief counseling session in which the counselor reinforced the client for the appropriate verbal statements (e.g., educational and vocational information-seeking behaviors). These behaviors were also the dependent or outcome variables for these four studies. Two control groups were also used in each of the four studies. Similar results were found in all four studies: 1) both treatments (reinforcement and model-reinforcement) were equally more effective than no treatment, 2) both treatments were equally effective for female clients, and 3) model-reinforcement counseling was more effective for male clients (the models used were males and topics of the taped sessions centered around male concerns and interests). Similar findings were obtained with students attending small rural high schools (Meyer, Strowig, and Hosford, 1970). Model-reinforcement counseling was compared with counselor verbal prompting plus reinforcement, role-playing plus reinforcement, and control conditions on the frequency of self-initiated action of ninety-four high-achieving tenth grade pupils (Atkinson, 1971). The results of this study revealed that counselor reinforcement combined with either verbal prompting or video-tape models was more effective in producing student self-initiated action than the other two procedures. In another study, modeling with reinforcement was compared to modeling without reinforcement and to control groups (which received no treatment) for one hundred and forty tenth and eleventh graders (LaFleur and Johnson, 1972). Treatment procedures were presented in written booklets with cartoon models. The number of modeled behaviors, knowledge of modeled behaviors, and interest in information-seeking behaviors were the dependent variables. Modeling without reinforcement was just as effective as modeling with reinforcement on all three dependent variables and both procedures were better than no treatment as received by the control groups. The authors concluded that mere presentation of a model may be the only stimulus necessary to produce the desired behavior for adolescents (LaFleur and Johnson, 1972). For counselors working in school settings, modeling seems to be a powerful and efficient method for promoting a variety of student behaviors. Depending on the behavior to be acquired, social modeling procedures may be used supplementary to or in place of verbal interview sessions.

In using modeling procedures, it is important for the behavioral counselor to determine whether the client is able to attend and to perceive accurately all of the facets of the model behavior. For example, in two studies with autistic children, it was necessary for the therapists to obtain the children's attention before modeling procedures could be introduced (Risley and Wolf, 1967; Lovaas, 1967). After attentional control was obtained in both of these studies, successful shaping and modeling procedures were initiated.

Social modeling may also be a therapeutically beneficial procedure in clinical settings. Only a few studies have reported the use of modeling procedures with adults. Wilson and Walters (1966) found that modeling procedures were effective in developing speech patterns of mute schizophrenics, and Goldstein and his associates (1973) were able to increase independent behaviors of psychiatric outpatients with modeling procedures.

Vicarious Extinction

Emotional responses and behaviors can be extinguished as well as acquired through modeling procedures. Vicarious extinction refers to a particular type of modeling procedure in which the client views a hierarchy of modeled events gradually approximating the stimulus event (e.g., a situation which evokes an undesirable emotional response such as fear). A crucial feature for the success of this procedure is the model's performance of the stimulus event without experiencing adverse consequences. Some modeled stimulus events on the hierarchy may elicit emotional reactions from the client during the viewing process. However, it is assumed that these emotional reactions will occur at a lower arousal level than an actual contact with the stimulus event would evoke.

Several studies reported by Bandura (1969) have found vicarious extinction to be a beneficial procedure in decreasing fear arousal responses in subjects with varying fears and at different age levels. Vicarious extinction using a live model with guided practice was somewhat more effective than symbolic modeling or systematic desensitization in extinguishing subjects' fear of snakes (Bandura, Blanchard, and Ritter, 1969). Similarly, Shaw and Thoresen (1974) found that multiple video-taped models coupled with imaginary client practice (having dental work completed) was successful for seventy-seven percent of dental phobic subjects, compared to forty-four percent of subjects treated by systematic desensitization. The authors concluded that "persons with severe avoidance behaviors and behavioral deficits may require very specific and repeated demonstrations of appropriate behavior along with various performance aids [Shaw and Thoresen, 1974, p. 12]."

Steps in Modeling Procedures

In using various modeling procedures in counseling, the overall effectiveness of modeling may be enhanced by the following considerations.

Developing Models

1. Identify the individual(s) for whom the model is intended. A complete identification would include age, sex, perceived socio-economic status level, school or work interests, ethnic variables, and types of potential reinforcers.
2. Identify (usually in conjunction with the client) the target behavior(s) to be acquired, strengthened, weakened, or extinguished. These behaviors should be stated in observable terms with a detailed description of any sub-behaviors required in performance of the overall goal (see "Establishing Goals" in Chapter 2).

3. Decide on the mode of model presentation. Select either a live model, a symbolic model, or a combination of both. In using live models to demonstrate behaviors, or actors and actresses to perform behaviors on tapes, the models should be practiced several times before presentation to the client. Live or symbolic models may be more potent when they are displayed in vivid, novel form. As an example, the use of humor, cartoons, and illustrations may heighten the perceived novelty of the model. Models should also be selected on the basis of their age, sex, status, and competency in relationship to the client. The effects of modeling are likely to be more powerful when multiple (several heterogeneous) models are presented who demonstrate the desired behaviors in a variety of ways.

4. Models can be presented in one of two different ways: a coping model or a mastery model. The coping model is a person who gradually attains the desired behavior and who shows the effort needed to perform the behaviors. In contrast, a mastery model initially displays all of the desired behaviors and does not demonstrate the effort required to master the skills. Some evidence suggests that coping models may be slightly more effective than mastery models because the client can observe both the behaviors to be acquired or weakened as well as possible ways to achieve the desired effect (Meichenbaum and Cameron, 1974).

Implementing Modeling Procedures

In implementing a modeling presentation with a client, the following procedural details should be noted.

1. The client's level of attention must be fully directed to the modeling stimuli. Therefore, before the model is presented, it is helpful to obtain the client's involvement with the model through directed focusing, relationship variables, or "gimmicks." In using a model with a client who, for one reason or another, appears to be very emotionally upset, the emotional level should be reduced before the model is presented.

2. The effects of modeling are likely to be greater when the client is presented with an expectancy set regarding the type of model and the modeling procedures (e.g., "You are about to see someone similar to yourself who is mastering the skill of effective study behaviors.").

3. Specific and detailed instructions presented prior to the model will assist the client in identifying the necessary components of the modeled behaviors.

4. The effects of modeling are likely to be greater when the presentation of the model is followed by opportunities to practice the modeled responses that approximate the modeled behavior.
5. The client may be more likely to attend to and imitate the model when the model is presented in a non-competitive and low-threat atmosphere. This kind of atmosphere may help to make the modeling process a rewarding rather than an aversive experience.

An example of a symbolic model presented by video-tape has been developed by Eisenberg and Delaney (1970). The video simulation tape contained six examples of the modeled behavior, followed by six stimuli to which the client or trainee could respond, followed by immediate feedback. Written and slide-tape examples of symbolic models with opportunities for practice and feedback have been developed by Cormier and Cormier (1974c). Regardless of the particular mode of the model presented, opportunities for the client to try out the response under low-threat conditions are essential in acquisition and retention of new behaviors and extinction of undesired responses. Note that the presence of a counselor is not a necessary condition for successful modeling. Once the model is developed, particularly in the case of symbolic presentations, the entire implementation can occur on a self-instructional basis. Social modeling can be a potentially efficient procedure.

Behavior Rehearsal

Behavior rehearsal, a word coined by Lazarus (1966), has sometimes been referred to as "behavioristic psychodrama" (Wolpe, 1958) or "role-play." However, behavior rehearsal, as used by Lazarus, has a specific meaning that differentiates behavior rehearsal from a role-play activity. Lazarus (1966, p. 209) defined behavior rehearsal as a "specific procedure which aims to replace deficient or interpersonal responses by efficient and effective behavior patterns. The patient achieves this by practicing the desired forms of behavior under the direction and supervision of the therapist."

Lazarus (1966, p. 209) reported some typical behavior patterns to which behavior rehearsal can be applied:

a. "I'm being interviewed for a job next week and I just don't know how to get across the fact that I really know my work although my qualifications are not as high as they should be."
b. "I keep putting off phoning Mary for a date because I don't know what to say to her."

   c. "I'm completely useless at starting conversations with strangers."

   d. "How can I get my husband to realize that if I take a morning job, the house and the children will not be neglected?"

   e. "In two weeks' time I'm having an oral test on counseling techniques. I wonder what sort of questions they can put to me?"

   f. "I never know what to say when people ask me questions about my daughter who is in a mental hospital."

Behavior rehearsal has three purposes: 1) the client can evaluate his/her present behaviors, 2) the new behaviors can be tried out by the client, and 3) the client can evaluate and/or identify the immediate consequences (usually on others) resulting from the new behaviors.

Kanfer and Phillips (1970, p. 187) pointed out that the extent to which an individual's observed behavior may change is a function of "1) an observation, 2) memory or storage, and 3) test for reproduction of observed behaviors." The specific elements of behavior rehearsal that contribute to the process of change need further clarification. However, several research studies have provided evidence to suggest that observation of a model, opportunity for live practice, and feedback are essential to the effectiveness of behavior rehearsal.

Early research evidence stemmed from applications of Moreno's "psychodrama" technique (1946), in which an individual was assigned a role to act out, usually with the intent of producing attitudinal and/or emotional change. Janis and Mann (1965) and Mann (1967) conducted a series of studies investigating the effects of types of role-play procedures on cigarette smoking. These studies indicated that role-play was more effective (i.e., produced greater changes in reduction of cigarette consumption) for groups that had an "emotional" or live role-play experience in which subjects were told they had lung cancer and were instructed to experience pain and early death. The groups experiencing this "emotional" role-play strategy were more affected than the control groups and those groups who experienced "cognitive" role-play in which the advantages and hazards of smoking were discussed (Janis and Mann, 1965; Mann, 1967). Furthermore, factual information about the hazards of smoking did not reduce the participants' level of smoking, although it did enhance the effects of the role-play procedure (Mann and Janis, 1968). These findings support Bandura's (1969) evidence that live participation is an essential component in elimination of behavioral deficits and in acquisition of new responses. Consequently, the probability of the client's experiencing success with a new behavior pattern in the environmental setting is increased.

Several researchers have investigated the efficacy of behavior rehearsal in therapeutic settings. In these studies, behavior rehearsal has produced significantly more behavior change on the dependent variables than the therapeutic techniques of 1) reflection-interpretation and 2) advice-giving. For example, Lazarus (1966) completed a comparative study of 1) reflection-interpretation, 2) advice, and 3) behavior rehearsal in effecting behavior change (defined as observable action outside of the interview) for seventy-five patients. Lazarus found that in the "behavior rehearsal" group, ninety-two percent of the clients changed, while thirty-two percent changed in the reflection-interpretation group, and forty percent changed in the advice-giving group. Lazarus (1966, p. 212) concluded that "behavioral rehearsal is significantly more effective in resolving specific social and interpersonal problems than direct advice or nondirective therapy." However, the results should be interpreted carefully since Lazarus administered all three treatments, and the possibility of experimenter bias may pose a threat to the validity of the study.

McFall and Marston (1970) conducted an investigation of the effects of behavior rehearsal in assertive training of forty-two "non-assertive" college undergraduate volunteer subjects. The subjects were assigned randomly to two experimental conditions and two control conditions. The experimental conditions were 1) behavior rehearsal *with* performance feedback, and 2) behavior rehearsal *without* feedback. The control conditions were 1) placebo insight therapy, and 2) waiting-list-no-treatment control. In all three of the dependent variable measures (behavior, self-report, and autonomic), the subjects in the behavior rehearsal groups showed significantly more positive change than the subjects in the control groups. Furthermore, the behavior of the subjects who received performance feedback as a part of behavior rehearsal changed more. Not only did behavior rehearsal seem to be more effective than no treatment, but the added component of *feedback* appeared to enhance the behavior change.

McFall and Lillesand (1971) compared the effects of two types of behavior rehearsal (overt and covert) with a control group on one aspect of assertive behavior: the ability to refuse (say "no") to engage in an unreasonable request. Thirty-three college undergraduate volunteer subjects were assigned randomly to one of three conditions: 1) *overt* behavior rehearsal with *modeling* and *coaching,* 2) *covert* behavior rehearsal with *modeling* and *coaching,* and

3) placebo-control. On the general measures, no differences were found between the treatment and control subjects. On every specific measure of refusal behavior, the treatment subjects improved significantly more than the control subjects, whose behavior remained essentially unchanged. These researchers also found that covert behavior rehearsal was as effective and, on some measures, more effective than overt rehearsal. Thus, a major implication for using behavior rehearsal as a counseling strategy is that counselors have two types of behavior rehearsal procedures available for use with clients: 1) *overt*, in which the client rehearses the response aloud, and 2) *covert*, in which the client imagines and reflects on the response. Some clients may find the covert rehearsal more useful since it may be less threatening. Other clients may benefit from the overt rehearsal, in that it permits greater monitoring and feedback from the counselor.

Implementation of Behavior Rehearsal

The strategies and results of the previously reported research studies suggest that the following steps should be considered in the application of behavior rehearsal (Cormier and Cormier, 1974d).

1. The counselor and the client specify the problem situation and identify the behaviors to be acquired in the situation. This may occur verbally or in a "role-repetition" manner in which the client enacts his/her typical behaviors in the situation. Behaviors to be acquired are identified from this performance.

2. The counselor takes the part of the client and models the identified behavior in a simulated version of the situation.

3. The client is asked to identify verbally the specific behaviors performed by the counselor in the rehearsal demonstration. (If the client is unable to do so, step 2 should be completed again.)

4. Simulating the situation again, the client takes his/her own part and tries out the target behavior. This can be accomplished in an *overt* rehearsal in which the client actually demonstrates the specified responses, or in a *covert* manner in which the client imagines engaging in the identified behavior.

5. The counselor gives the client feedback about her/his performance. The counselor praises positive aspects of the client's performance and identifies behaviors the client should include in another rehearsal. Additional feedback can be provided to the client via an audio- or video-recording of the rehearsal.

6. Practice of the behavior occurs again either overtly, where the

client practices the behavior in view of the counselor, or covertly, where the client imagines engaging in the behavior. Continuous feedback and behavior rehearsal occurs until the client can perform or can imagine the behavior successfully and without anxiety.

Behavior rehearsal can be adapted for use in group settings as well as dyadic counseling. The group environment can provide the cues for elicitation of new behavior as well as multiple sources of feedback to strengthen behavior change. As will be seen in the next section, behavior rehearsal is also an important component in assertive training.

Assertive Training

With non-assertive clients, assertive training can be described as a process of arranging environmental conditions so that certain impulses that may have been previously inhibited by anxiety can be expressed in overt behavior (Krumboltz and Thoresen, 1969). With clients who report difficulty due to aggressive behavior, assertive training involves having the client distinguish between agressive and assertive behaviors and rehearse assertive behaviors for situations that have usually evoked aggressive responses.

Counselors who use assertive training may regard non-assertive or aggressive behavior as the result of a history of maladaptive habit formation. Wolpe (1958) hypothesized that in the case of a non-assertive individual, assertive behavior can be used to inhibit anxiety, since a person cannot be assertive and anxious at the same time. This hypothesis has been empirically supported in a study conducted by Goldstein, Serber, and Piaget (1970), who reduced fear in three subjects through the artificial induction of anger as an inhibitor of anxiety.

In using assertive training with clients, one of the important steps involves a specific identification of the maladaptive behaviors expressed by the client and of the more appropriate behaviors the client would like to learn. Consequently, an important distinction should be made between non-assertive, assertive, and aggressive behaviors (Alberti and Emmons, 1970).

Types of Assertive Responses

Three studies (Mischel, 1968; McFall and Marston, 1970; Hersen, Eisler, and Miller, 1973) have investigated the nature of assertive behavior. These investigations found little evidence to support the notion of assertiveness as a generalized response or personality trait. The studies suggested that assertiveness may be more accurately described as a broad, heterogeneous, and situation-specific response class (McFall and Marston, 1970). In other words, assertiveness may be defined as any number of assertive kinds of behaviors, specific to certain stimulus conditions. Consequently, in using assertive training with clients, the counselor should identify both *verbal* and *nonverbal* types of responses.

Rathus (1972) reported nine kinds of verbal assertive behaviors, adapted from "excitatory exercises" prescribed by Salter (1949). These are examples of some verbal assertive behaviors: expression of opinions, expression of feelings, "greeting talk," expression of active disagreement, asking why, talking about oneself, agreeing with compliments, and avoiding the justification of opinions. Another example of verbal assertive behavior could be refusal to carry out an unreasonable request.

Equally important in developing assertive behavior is the paralinguistic component of assertive responses. Consideration must be given to how the message is delivered in addition to the type of message being sent. Serber (1972) has categorized nonverbal elements of assertive behavior into six different categories: loudness of voice (pitch), fluency of spoken words (rate and coherence of speech), eye contact, facial expression, body expression (position and gestures), and distance from the person with whom one is interacting (proxemics).

The literature contains several reports of empirical investigations of assertive training. Generally, all reported studies have found assertive training to be an effective strategy in producing some changes in the assertive behavior under investigation. McFall and Marston (1970) and McFall and Lillesand (1971) reported significant changes in some assertive behaviors as a function of behavior rehearsal and assertive training.

Rathus (1972) conducted an investigation of assertive training in groups. His results showed that the assertive training subjects reported significantly greater gains in assertive behavior than did the control subjects, though the gains between the assertive training subjects and discussion only subjects were not statistically significant. Rathus (1973b) also compared assertive training using video-tape mediated assertive models with a placebo treatment and a control treatment. He reported that assertive training was more effective than either the placebo or control treatment in inducing more assertive behavior in his sample of undergraduate college women (Rathus, 1973b). Another study investigated the effectiveness of a multi-faceted group assertive training (Galassi, Galassi, and Litz, 1974). The assertive training consisted of video-tape modeling, behavior rehearsal, video-taped peer and trainee feedback, bibliotherapy, and homework assignments. Significant differences were found between the assertive training groups and the control groups on the College Self-Expression Scale and on role-play situations. The above reported research suggests that assertive training can be an effective counseling strategy in both dyadic and group settings.

Two other studies have investigated the effects of assertive training with a group of hospitalized patients and with a group of outpatients (Lomont, Gilner, Spector, and Skinner, 1969; Bloomfield, 1973). The first study compared group assertive training with group insight therapy on the clinical scales of the MMPI (Lomont, et al., 1969). These groups met for six weeks, and the results indicate that the assertive training group showed a significantly greater total decrease than the insight group on the MMPI clinical scales with significant decreases on the depression and anxiety scales. In the second study, Bloomfield (1973) reported "successful" outcomes (e.g., increasing the range of interpersonal skills and decreasing social anxiety) of assertive training with outpatients. However, it is difficult to determine the validity of the effects of assertive training because within-subject (baseline data) comparisons were not reported.

The reader may note a strong similarity between the assertive training strategy and the behavior rehearsal procedure described in the previous section. Overt and covert behavior rehearsal is one of the primary components of assertive training. In four studies assessing the relative contributions of components of assertive training, McFall and Twentyman (1973) found that rehearsal and coaching made significant additive contributions to performance on self-report and behavioral assertion measures. In the same four studies, symbolic models of assertive behavior added little to performance of the subjects. The modeling component was relatively unimportant regardless of the type of model presented (tactful versus abrupt) or the media used to present the model (audio-visual versus auditory only) (McFall and Twentyman, 1973). A description of the steps and sequence of assertive training is presented in the following section.

Steps in Assertive Training

Although the practice of assertive training may contain a number of different components, a typical assertive training procedure may be described as follows (Cormier and Cormier, 1974e):

1. The counselor and client must identify the *circumstances* or the *situation* in which the assertiveness is desired. Also, the client must specify the *verbal* and *nonverbal* behaviors that are presently occurring in the identified situation. It is not sufficient to describe the problem as "lack of assertiveness" or to describe the client as "overly aggressive."

2. Following accurate identification of the problem, the second step of assertive training requires selection of *goals*. Based upon the present behaviors identified in a situation in Step 1, the client might want to increase or decrease certain behaviors. For example, a client who reports instances of non-assertiveness would probably desire to increase the intensity and frequency of certain behaviors. In contrast, a client who reports instances of aggressive responses would most likely desire to decrease the intensity and frequency of certain behaviors.

3. The counselor (or a pre-recorded audio tape) uses instructional coaching to help the client identify alternative assertive behaviors desired in the problem situation. In coaching, the counselor suggests effective behavior in specific problem situations (e.g., "A good way to handle this situation is to be firm once you've refused to work overtime and don't give in.").

4. For a complex series of alternative behaviors, these responses can be arranged in a hierarchy, from behaviors that the client can achieve easily and successfully to those that may be more difficult to attain. After generating alternative behaviors and, at times, arranging these in a hierarchy, the counselor and client should select and agree upon the specific desired assertive behaviors.

5. The counselor models (or uses someone else or a video-tape as a model) the desired assertive behavior by taking the part of the client, and by demonstrating more effective behavior in the identified problem situation (the role reversal strategy).

6. The counselor introduces behavior rehearsal; the client now takes his/her own part again and begins to practice the desired assertive responses in the identified situation.

7. The counselor provides feedback to the client about his/her behavior; both the counselor and client evaluate the rehearsal. The counselor reinforces small steps of progress but also points out areas in which the client needs additional improvement. The counselor's feedback should include identification of specific behaviors. After evaluation of the rehearsal, the counselor and client need to decide if re-cycling of the modeling and rehearsal

steps is necessary or if the client is ready to apply the behaviors in the actual setting.

8. The client is ready at this point to apply his/her newly acquired assertive behaviors in "in vivo" or "real-life" situations. Assertive behavior tasks can be assigned for completion as homework outside of the interview. It is again important to utilize the concept of "successive approximations"; the client should engage in one or two small tasks at first that are relatively nonthreatening so that positive consequences are likely to occur.

9. The client should make an immediate report (in person or by telephone) to the counselor as soon as possible after engaging in the actual situation. The counselor should reward any degree of success experienced by the client, but also should help the client to understand the importance of continuous self-reinforcement. The client can draw on his/her own resources for engaging in assertive behaviors by identifying the positive outcomes and feelings resulting from assertive behaviors. After this "check-in," the counselor and the client will need to decide if the client needs to recycle or repeat any of the steps of the assertive training procedure. If not, the client may wish to apply assertive training to other behaviors (these may be specified in the hierarchy described under Step 4) or else may decide to terminate the counseling process.

The three behavioral counseling procedures of social modeling (with the exception of vicarious extinction), behavior rehearsal, and assertive training can facilitate the acquisition and strengthening of a client's behavior. In contrast, the procedures described in the following four sections are used primarily to decrease or eliminate an undesired behavior, such as anxiety. These procedures include systematic desensitization, flooding, implosion, and aversive therapy.

Systematic Desensitization

Systematic desensitization may well be one of the most prominent techniques associated with behavioral counseling. A quick perusal of the major behavioral counseling books and related journals reveals that desensitization is a frequently used therapeutic procedure. Systematic desensitization is a procedure in which a response incompatible with anxiety is paired with the anxiety response for the purpose of weakening the anxiety response. As defined originally by Wolpe (1958), the desensitization procedure consists of three major elements: 1) training in deep muscle relaxation (an incompatible response with anxiety), 2) construction of hierarchies consisting of items representing anxiety-evoking stimuli, and 3) graduated pairing, through imagery, of the items on the hierarchy with the relaxed state of the client.

Systematic desensitization was originally developed for use with phobias, in which a client had learned an anxiety response to a particular set of stimuli, such as school, airplanes, etc. More recently, desensitization has also been applied to test anxiety and to interpersonal anxiety, although some evidence indicates that the procedure may work best for monosymptomatic responses (Lang and Lazovik, 1963: Lazarus, 1971) rather than free-floating or prevalent anxiety states.

Bandura (1969) conceptualized anxiety or neurotic behavior as a persistent learned maladaptive behavior resulting from stimuli that have acquired the capacity to elicit high intensity emotional responses. As can be recalled from the discussion of classical conditioning in Chapter 1, fear may be considered a reflexive response (already existing within the client's repertoire). Many clients who report phobic fears have acquired a fear response to specific situations through the association or pairing that occurs in a classical conditioning paradigm of learning. In systematic desensitization, the fear response is weakened through counterconditioning by associating a neutral or anxiety-inhibiting stimulus with the unconditioned stimulus (the situation in which the client's anxiety response is evoked).

As conceived by Wolpe (1958), systematic desensitization was a counterconditioning procedure based on what he termed the "reciprocal inhibition principle." According to Wolpe's original statement, the ability of given stimuli to evoke anxiety will be weakened or eliminated if "a response antagonistic to anxiety can be made to occur in the presence of anxiety-evoking stimuli so that it is accompanied by a complete or partial suppression of the anxiety responses [1958, p. 71]."

The therapeutic process of desensitization is a graduated or progressive process, which is begun by pairing a response incompatible with anxiety, such as relaxation, with an anxiety-evoking stimulus item that is low on the client's hierarchy; in other words, an item that does not evoke a great deal of anxiety. After the anxiety to this item no longer exists, the pairing continues with items higher on the hierarchy. Usually, the items are all *imagined* by the client rather than carried out in an "in vivo" or actual setting. By beginning with a low item on the hierarchy, the incompatible anxiety response, such as relaxation, is dominant and inhibits the weak or low-level anxiety response, thereby establishing a learned inhibition of the anxiety response to a stimulus that typically elicited the anxiety. According to the reciprocal inhibition principle, after repeated presentations or pairings of the relaxation and the anxiety-evoking items, the anxiety responses to the situation are counter-conditioned and can no longer be elicited by this situation.

Although systematic desensitization has been empirically demonstrated to be effective in reduction of anxiety responses, some recent studies have challenged the theoretical basis of reciprocal inhibition as postulated by Wolpe (1958). The present controversy over systematic desensitization does not center around the effectiveness of the procedure but rather the mechanisms responsible for producing the anxiety reduction. Wilkins (1971, p. 311) has suggested that the effectiveness of desensitization may be due more to "social variables involved in the patient-therapist relationship and cognitive variables involving expectancy of therapeutic gain, information feedback of success, training in the control of attention, and vicarious learning of the contingencies of behavior through instructed imagination." Other studies have also cited the role of instructions (Oliveau, Agras, Leitenberg, Moore, and Wright, 1969) and feedback to the client (Riddick and Mayer, 1973) as important variables in the desensitization process. Such factors as patient-therapist relationship, expectancy of therapeutic gain, and information feedback have not been operative factors in effective demonstrations of self-instructed or programmed desensitization in which the client did not receive any interpersonal contact, expectancy set, or feedback results. Morgan has recently challenged the assumptions of Wilkins (1971):

> . . . In the absence of direct demonstrations, to claim that these are "critical variables" for successful therapeutic outcome in desensitization seems to go considerably beyond the data available, and, to suggest that the major operations of Wolpe's systematic desensitization procedure are not useful in the actual treatment of severely fearful patients would be quite premature [Morgan, 1973, p. 375].

Valins and Ray (1967) suggested that relaxation in the presence of disturbing images may enable the client to reassess the cognitive meaning of a situation in such a way that subsequent anxiety in that situation is reduced. Bandura (1969) has also acknowledged the role of cognitions in the anxiety reduction of a mildly anxious individual, but questioned the significance of a cognitive mechanism for reducing anxiety of those individuals with intense fears and well established avoidance behaviors. Other theorists have speculated that fear reduction in systematic desensitization may be due more to extinction than to counterconditioning, since the client is presented with repeated non-reinforced exposure to an aversive situation (Lomont, 1965; Wilson, 1973).

Demonstration of Effects of Systematic Desensitization

The outcomes of systematic desensitization, both in terms of client gain and empirical support, have been widely documented (Paul, 1969a and b). Generally, the procedure has been useful in counterconditioning phobias and in reducing academic and interpersonal anxieties. Marquis, Morgan, and Piaget (1973) have reported that frequent themes appearing in hierarchies involve criticism or rejection, fear of being the center of attention or public speaking, suffering and death, violence or anger, anxiety about specific people, shyness over courtship and sex, and work anxieties. Desensitization has been successfully used with diverse age groups (young children through adults), in individual and group settings, and by shortened or massed applications of the procedure.

Case Studies

Wolpe (1961) reported seventy-eight out of eighty-five surveyed cases as treatment successes. Treatment success was defined by at least an eighty percent reduction of anxiety and related maladaptive behaviors. The only consistent evidence used by Wolpe (1961) was patient self-report. These cases included interpersonal and situational anxieties, complex phobias, depression and feelings of inferiority, impotence, frigidity, and stuttering.

For two hundred and twenty cases receiving more than one desensitization session, Lazarus (1967) reported one hundred and ninety as treatment successes. Lazarus solicited external reports as well as client self-reports on a five-point scale. Pre- and post-treatment scores on the Willoughby scale, Bernreuter scale, and Maudsley Personality Inventory were also taken into account. Numerous other uncontrolled case studies have reported the use of systematic desensitization, including school phobia (Garvey and Hegrenes, 1966), airplane phobia (Scrignar, Swanson, and Bloom, 1973), exhibitionism (Bond and Hutchinson, 1960), frigidity (Madsen and Ullmann, 1967), public speaking anxiety (Hosford, 1969a), and interpersonal problems (Gelder and Marks, 1966). A detailed report is available in Paul's (1969a and b) thorough summary of the outcomes of systematic desensitization. One major methodological problem of these reports involves bias in client self-reports and disagreement among the therapists regarding criteria of success. Also, lack of control data makes it impossible to screen out other effects that may have partially accounted for treatment success.

Controlled Studies

The first controlled study of systematic desensitization was reported by Lang and Lazovik (1963) with college undergraduate subjects who reported intense fears of non-poisonous snakes on the Fear Survey Schedule. The study utilized two treatment and two control groups. The treatment groups were involved in five sessions of relaxation training and eleven sessions of desensitization. At the end of the relaxation training period, no significant differences were found between the desensitization and the control groups. However, on the post-treatment assessment, following the eleven sessions of desensitization, the treatment subjects showed significantly greater reductions in avoidance of the snake than did the control subjects. This study was the first to establish a cause-effect relationship between the application of systematic desensitization and change in maladaptive responses. This relationship was later demonstrated in a study in which desensitization was significantly more effective than an insight-oriented treatment and an attention-placebo treatment in all physiological measures of public speaking anxiety (Paul, 1966). These treatment results, as well as greater evidence of significant generalization effects, were reported in a two-year follow-up of the original subjects (Paul, 1967). Later studies have established cause-effect evidence for the application of systematic desensitization in tension-produced respiratory problems (Moore, 1965) and in reduction of test anxiety among university students (Emery and Krumboltz, 1967; Donner and Guerney, 1969; Graff, MacLean, and Loving, 1971; Osterhouse, 1972; Allen, 1971; and Cornish and Dilley, 1973). Reduction of test anxiety has also been achieved through systematic desensitization with elementary school children (Barabasz, 1972) and junior high school students (Mann and Rosenthal, 1969; Mann, 1972). Recent controlled studies have indicated the effectiveness of desensitization in reducing math anxiety (Suinn, Edie, and Spinelli, 1970; Richardson and Suinn, 1973), in reducing fear of contact with members of the opposite sex (Dua, 1972), and in reducing interpersonal anxiety while increasing the acquisition of facilitative communication skills (Fry, 1973). All of these studies have been conducted with college or adult subjects which limits generalizability of the findings to other populations.

One of the major methodological problems of all of the controlled studies has been lack of standardized assessment procedures for changes in behavior and anxiety. As Franks observed (1970), most of the studies in which anxiety reduction was the dependent variable used different definitions of anxiety and different instruments to measure anxiety. Davison (1965) observed that changes in behavior can occur without accompanying anxiety reduction, just as changes in responses to attitudinal questionnaires may not necessarily reflect changes in anxiety. Future researchers investigating systematic desensitization must agree on reliable physiological indices of anxiety (Franks, 1970) and upon the development of "standardized assessment procedures with adequate reliability and validity [Paul, 1969b, p. 159]."

Variations of Systematic Desensitization

Recent studies have departed from the original studies in which systematic desensitization was applied in a package tailored for an individual client and administered in the context of a one-to-one therapeutic relationship. Variations of the systematic desensitization procedure include applications in group settings, massing of the procedure over a short time, automated self-administered desensitization, and variations in hierarchy presentation and imagery procedures.

Application in Groups

The first report in which desensitization was applied in a group setting was published by Lazarus (1961). Desensitization was administered in a group consisting of phobic subjects, with use of a single hierarchy directed toward the major phobia. On subject self-reports and tolerance tests, group desensitization was more successful than was the treatment for two interpretation therapy groups. Paul and Shannon (1966) extended the group desensitization approach to the treatment of social-evaluative anxiety. Relaxation training and hierarchies were standardized for all subjects in the group desensitization treatment. The desensitization group, compared to a control group, showed significant anxiety reduction in "target" areas of desensitization and on related interpersonal-anxiety scales as well. Desensitization was reported to be effective in a group of twenty college students using standardized group-administered relaxation procedures and test anxiety hierarchy (Graff, et al., 1971), and in small groups of elementary students (Barabasz, 1972) and junior high studens (Deffenbacher and Kemper, 1974). In an innovative study involving group desensitization with adults, Fry (1973) conducted training in the core facilitative conditions of empathy, respect, concreteness, and genuineness (Carkhuff, 1969) for two treatment groups. The second group received additional training consisting of desensitization to anxiety in interpersonal intimacy. A standardized hierarchy of four areas — tone of voice, facial expressions, eye contact, and posture — was administered to all subjects in this group. The group who had received desensitization showed greater improvement in the level of core conditions than the group who had only received core condition communication training. This study demonstrates the effectiveness of desensitization in groups, and suggests another potential use of the procedure — as a training adjunct to reduce fear and defensiveness in individuals designated as "helpers."

Massed Desensitization

The studies involving the application of systematic desensitization in group settings have reported the efficiency and economy of the procedure, both for client and counselor, as one of its major advantages. In an effort to speed up the treatment effects, more recent investigations have attempted to determine the effectiveness of desensitization in "massed" intervals of time. Suinn, et al. (1970) compared the effects of a marathon desensitization group with an accelerated mass desensitization group (AMDG) on reduction of math anxiety of college undergraduates as measured by the Math Anxiety Rating Scale (MARS) and the math form of the Differential Aptitude Test (DAT). Both groups received one hour of relaxation training. The marathon group received five additional treatment blocks in a four-hour period during one night. This group worked progressively through each item on a group hierarchy. The accelerated group, in a two hour period in one evening, worked only on the highest (most anxiety-evoking) items on the hierarchy. Both groups improved equally on the two measures of math anxiety. In a later study utilizing the same two measures of math anxiety with college undergraduates, Richardson and Suinn (1973) compared the effectiveness of group desensitization over a three-week period and an accelerated massed desensitization group with a control group. The accelerated group received one hour of relaxation training, three hours of desensitization, and completed only the highest items on the hierarchy. Both the group desensitization and the accelerated group improved significantly on the self-report math anxiety scale (MARS) compared to the control group. A comparison of three massing desensitization procedures conducted in groups of college undergraduates was reported by Dua (1972). The dependent variable, reduction of fear of physical contact, was assessed by a self-report Fear Survey Scale and various behavioral tasks. The three massed intervals consisted of five one-hour sessions 1) over a twelve-hour period, 2) over a five-day period, and 3) over a fifteen-day period. The results indicated that the twelve-hour and five-day massed subjects showed a greater improvement on the behavioral tasks, while the fifteen-day massed subjects reported a greater anxiety reduction on the Fear Survey Scale. The limited evidence available on accelerated massed applications of systematic desensitization suggests that this technique may result in anxiety reduction within a very short time span. However, specific time spans may vary in effectiveness for different types of anxiety and other client variables. Until further replication is conducted, the specific potentialities of massed applications remain relatively unknown.

Self-Administered Desensitization

Another variation of the desensitization procedure designed to conserve counselor time involves the use of automated, client-administered desensitization. Typically the client administers the treatment with the use of a written manual or with standardized audio-tapes, many of which are presently available commercially (Dawley and Wenrich, 1973). Other studies (Marquis and Morgan, 1968; Donner and Guerney, 1969; Nawas, Fishman and Pucel, 1970; Cornish and Dilley, 1973) indicate that, for many clients, the presence of the counselor may not be a necessary element in the success of desensitization. Variations of self-administered desensitization have included techniques in which the client uses self-administered relaxation skills and pairs the relaxation with the onset of any physiological stress cues (Suinn and Richardson, 1971). Relaxation skills have been used as self-management procedures in stressful situations (Sherman and Plummer, 1973) and in the reduction of insomnia (Weil and Goldfried, 1973). Implosive therapy has also been administered by a packaged set of audio-taped instructions (Cornish and Dilley, 1973). Other self-administered procedures that can reduce anxiety include meditation (Maupin, 1969; Berwick and O'Zeil, 1973) and autogenic training (Luthe, 1969).

Procedural Variations

Many other studies have reported variations in the procedures of desensitization, particularly in the mode and format of hierarchy presentation. Standardized hierarchies have been found to be as effective as individual hierarchies (Emery and Krumboltz, 1967; McGlynn, Wilson, and Linder, 1970). Actual role-play of the hierarchy items has been reported in place of imagery (Hosford, 1969a). Items have also been presented through slides rather than imagery

(Goldberg and D'Zurilla, 1968). Use of slides or role-play may be more effective for clients who report difficulty in initiating and maintaining the covert images. Imagery of items was compared to slide presentation of items and to enactment of scenes "in vivo" for both behavioral tasks and self-report measures of snake phobic male subjects. All three groups reduced reports of fear and improved on behavioral tasks. After a three week follow-up, the third group, who had enacted the scenes "in vivo," achieved the greatest anxiety reduction (O'Neil and Howell, 1969). "Contact" desensitization has also been reported, in which the client is exposed to a model who demonstrates the desired behavior. In contact desensitization, the client also enacts the items by demonstrating the desired behavior in graduated increments (Ritter, 1968). These studies lend support to Franks and Wilson's (1973, p. 75) contention that emphasis in systematic desensitization procedures should be on "graded real-life encounters with the feared situation . . . since behavior, including avoidance behavior, is probably most effectively modified in the actual environment in which it occurs."

Other innovations in hierarchy construction and presentation have been proposed by Hekmat (1972), Staats (1972), and Meichenbaum (1974). Hekmat and Staats have described *semantic* desensitization, in which the client uses positive words as images in response to certain problem stimulus words that would ordinarily center around the theme of the hierarchy items. This procedure is designed to eliminate the conditioned negative words or images that have become associated with the target stimulus.

Meichenbaum (1974) suggests that an alternative to the systematic desensitization process described by Wolpe (1958) may involve teaching the client a set of coping skills to foster self control. Meichenbaum expanded the desensitization process to include a set of "coping images" visualized by the client. The coping imagery requires the client to imagine becoming anxious and then to imagine handling the anxiety by means of slow, deep breaths and self-instructional coping statements that are incompatible with anxiety. Meichenbaum points out that the actual visualization of "coping images" may assist the client in mentally rehearsing the specific cognitions and behaviors he/she will use in stressful situations. Meichenbaum noted that the positive results of the coping imagery process are based on preliminary research, but the evidence for this process is accumulating in different areas, including the use of coping imagery to reduce fears of phobic clients (Meichenbaum, 1974) and to teach clients how to cope with pain (Turk, 1974).

While the controlled studies suggest a variety of alternative applications of systematic desensitization, some of the evidence is confounded by a wide range of reported procedural variations. Since the procedures define the independent variable, such variability limits the generalization of the results. In a critical review of the existing experimental studies, Paul and Trimble (1970, p. 286) noted that:

> Random variability of procedures in any of the three major components of systematic desensitization may introduce differences such that generalization of findings from one investigation to another, or from controlled research to clinical practice may be inappropriate or unwarranted. In fact, many published papers report such deviant procedures that the relationship to current evidence regarding systematic desensitization is, at best, tangential.

Paul (1969b, p. 159) has recommended that future research focus on "appropriate process studies to determine the mechanisms of operation" and on "parametric studies to standardize and operationalize the most efficient procedures for individuals and groups." While systematic desensitization is one of the first psychotherapeutic procedures in history to withstand and undergo rigorous evaluation, a wealth of hypotheses are still untested (Paul, 1969b).

Steps in Systematic Desensitization Procedures

Some of the most recent concrete descriptions of desensitization procedures that may be useful for the behavioral counselor are reported by Marquis, Morgan, and Piaget (1973); Krumboltz and Thoresen (1969, in press); Dustin and George (1973); and Rimm and Masters (1974). A well-described presentation of the variables of systematic desensitization was provided by Marquis et al. (1973). The steps associated with systematic desensitization are described as follows:

1. The first step, conducting a behavioral analysis, is carried out primarily to identify the client's problem, to identify the parameters of the anxiety experienced by the client, and to identify a client for whom desensitization may be inappropriate. The procedures suggested for problem identification in Chapter 2 can be applied here to assist clients in identifying specific anxiety-evoking stimuli.

2. An adequate behavioral analysis sets the stage for the next step, construction of a hierarchy. While items on a hierarchy may be generated through counselor-client verbal report, a client can also keep track of anxiety-evoking stimuli on note cards which later can be added to the hierarchy and arranged in a graduated order with questioning and cueing by the counselor. The hierarchy used in

desensitization consists of ten to twenty descriptive items representing parameters of the anxiety-evoking stimuli. The items are arranged in a graduated order from the lowest or least anxiety-producing item to the highest or most anxiety-producing item. The items are graduated or spaced successively in one of several ways, and can be constructed from low-anxious to high-anxious on one of several dimensions. In selecting items for a hierarchy, Marquis et al. (1973) suggest three important considerations: 1) items should represent real experiences of the client and should be described in ways that are realistic for the individual client, 2) items should contain enough details in the description to facilitate the imagery process by the client, and 3) items should encompass the entire domain in which the fear might operate and include stimuli that are likely to elicit all levels of anxiety, from low to high.

Hierarchies may be defined along spatial-temporal dimensions, thematic dimensions, or personal dimensions (Marquis et al., 1973). The type of hierarchy constructed can easily influence the kind and degree of outcome of the desensitization procedure (Morgan, 1973). Many experimental studies have utilized a spatial-temporal hierarchy, while counselors may prefer a thematic hierarchy. The particular type of hierarchy will depend on the client's problem and preference. The spatial-temporal hierarchy consists of items along physical and/or time dimensions, such as distance from a phobic object or time remaining before getting married. This type of hierarchy may be particularly useful to reduce anxiety to a particular event, an object, or a person. Thematic hierarchies consist of graduated items representing the different parameters of the anxiety-producing situation. For example, a client's anxiety in interpersonal situations may vary with the setting, number of people, sex of the persons, degree of prior acquaintance, and so forth. In using this type of hierarchy, it may be necessary to desensitize the client to each specific component before combining the parameters for an overall desensitization procedure. Personal hierarchies may be used to desensitize the client to constant memories or uncomfortable ruminations of a specific individual. Dengrove (1966) suggested that this method is often very effective in desensitizing anxiety produced by loss-related situations (e.g., loss of a job) or dissolution of a relationship through death, divorce, defection, or geographical separation. This type of hierarchy could also be used to countercondition a client's avoidance behavior to a particular person who, because of punitive interactions, has become aversive to the client. The lowest items on the hierarchy can represent pleasant interactions while the higher items can represent more anxiety-producing or aversive interactions. Some valuable illustrations of various types of hierarchies are presented in *A Guidebook to Systematic Desensitization* (Marquis, Morgan, and Piaget, 1973).

Together the counselor and client can arrange the items in the hierarchy with appropriate spacing between items. There are four possible methods of scaling and spacing items on a hierarchy: rank-ordering, subjective unit of disturbance (suds) scaling, equal-appearing intervals, and just-noticeable differences (Marquis et al., 1973). One of the most popular spacing methods involves distribution of items along a zero to one hundred-point continuum. Each item is placed at a particular point along the scale of "suds" or "subjective units of disturbance" (Wolpe and Lazarus, 1966). Zero indicates complete relaxation while one hundred, at the other end of the continuum, represents complete panic. An interesting variation in the use of "suds" has been proposed by Sherman and Cormier (1972), who suggested using "suds" to quantify levels of interpersonal reactions, such as subjective units of anger (sua) in family counseling or subjective units of irritation (sui) in teacher-student relationships. Although hierarchy construction should be carried out carefully, it should be viewed as tentative until it is actually used in the desensitization process. Often in the middle of desensitization it may be necessary to add, delete, or change positions of items on the hierarchy.

3. In the third step associated with the desensitization procedure, a response incompatible with anxiety must be selected to be paired with the items on the hierarchy. A typically incompatible response has been relaxation, since a client cannot be relaxed and anxious at the same time. However, other anxiety inhibiting responses have also been used, including aggressive responses (Goldstein, Serber, and Piaget, 1970), assertive responses (Wolpe, 1958), sexual behavior (Clopton and Risbrough, 1973), laughter (Ventis, 1973), emotive imagery (Lazarus and Abramovitz, 1962), food (Wolpe and Lazarus, 1966), and, with children, toys and parental body contact (Bentler, 1962). These responses may be used for a client who has difficulty in achieving a state of relaxation when a hierarchy item is being carried out "in vivo" and prevents relaxation, or when there is not sufficient time to train a client in deep muscle relaxation. While it is possible to facilitate relaxation with drugs, such as quick-acting barbiturates, the preferred method is to train the client in deep muscle relaxation. Often this involves teaching the client the difference between tensed and relaxed muscle groups in the body (Jacobson, 1938) or having the client

imagine and attend to draining the tension from his/her body, beginning with the head and ending with the feet (Hosford, 1972). Other methods of relaxation are described in Lang and Lazovik (1960), Wolpe and Lazarus (1966), and Dawley and Wenrich (1973). While clients can be trained in relaxation skills in an automated manner with records or audio-tapes, feedback regarding the client's progress and level of relaxation may speed up the acquisition of these skills. Some studies indicate that clients may achieve fear reduction without prior training in relaxation (Rachman, 1968; Mann, 1972). Schubot (1966) demonstrated that relaxation was an essential component in modifying the fears of highly fearful subjects but was not an important element in fear reduction of only moderately fearful subjects. Using desensitization without a competing response such as relaxation will depend primarily on the client's baseline level of reported anxiety. After the client has been trained in relaxation or some other anxiety-inhibiting response, and after the purpose and process of desensitization has been explained, the pairing process can begin.

4. The pairing process in systematic desensitization may be summarized in the following steps:

a) The counselor presents the first item on the hierarchy to the client and describes what the client should imagine.

b) After several seconds, if the client does not signal anxiety (usually by raising the index finger) the counselor instructs the client to terminate the image and either relax or imagine a neutral, pleasant scene, such as sunbathing or sailing.

c) The counselor presents the same item again and asks the client to visualize the item for about twenty-five seconds. If the client does not signal anxiety, the second item on the hierarchy is presented.

d) This process is continued until an item is presented which evokes anxiety in the client. As soon as the client signals anxiety, he/she is instructed to terminate the image and to visualize a neutral or a pleasant scene, and continue relaxing. Inter-item relaxation visualization should continued for one to several minutes. Then the item is presented again. If the client does not signal anxiety, the next item on the hierarchy is presented.

Generally, if an item is presented three times and fails to elicit a no-anxiety response from the client, the counselor drops back to the preceding item on the hierarchy and also adds another item to the hierarchy that is a little less anxiety-provoking than the one that evoked client anxiety. Criterion for successful item completion is at least two no-anxiety repetitions. More than two presentations may be necessary for overlearning of the top items on the hierarchy. Since the last item of any learning series is well retained (Lazarus and Rachman, 1957), all sessions should end with an item that evokes no anxiety, even if it means returning to a previous item on the hierarchy.

Each desensitization session should begin with the last item successfully completed in the previous session, primarily to check for spontaneous recovery of the anxiety response. When this happens, the counselor will have to start again at the lower end of the hierarchy. Spontaneous recovery of anxiety may depend on timing of the desensitization process, including duration of scene presentation, inter-session intervals, and session duration. Typically, an item or scene presentation duration consists of fifteen to twenty seconds, although some recent evidence suggests that thirty- and forty-five-second duration prevents spontaneous recovery of previously desensitized items and results in more long-term anxiety reduction and faster desensitization of the items at the higher end of the hierarchy (Watts, 1973, 1974). Whether desensitization is conducted with a counselor or on a self-instructional basis by the client, it is important that records be kept regarding what items were completed, length of scene presentation, and other procedural details.

Limitations

While systematic desensitization is only one of several anxiety management techniques, failure of the process is often due to one of several variables within the process rather than the overall procedure. Some reasons for the ineffectiveness of desensitization may result from use of a wrong or incomplete hierarchy, inability of the client to engage in adequate visual imagery, and difficulty in achieving a desired level of relaxation or other anxiety-inhibiting response. When the procedure is applied effectively and still does not result in any measurable fear reduction, client variables may partially account for the inadequacy. These may include psychotic thought processes of some clients, cases where overt fears have secondary or symbolic attached phobias, or instances where, outside of counseling, the client is being reinforced for the anxiety reaction.

As Franks and Wilson (1973, p. 73) observed, "systematic desensitization has achieved a position of prominence and even eminence" as the "first demonstrably useful behavioral technique to be developed for the treatment of neurotic behavior." While a great deal of research has demonstrated the therapeutic value of desensitization in a wide variety of cases, the laboratory analogues will need verification for counseling and clinical practice. Moreover, in view of other anxiety management strategies, further research is needed to establish under what conditions, for what problems, and for what types of anxiety systematic desensitization may be the most effective and efficient behavioral counseling procedure.

Reactive Inhibition or Flooding

The principle of reciprocal inhibition as the mechanism of desensitization has recently been challenged by some individuals who contend that extinction rather than counterconditioning is responsible for any resulting fear reduction. As early as 1965, Lomont argued that desensitization may involve extinction operations as well as reinforcement of a new response that is incompatible with anxiety. In contrast to desensitization based on the reciprocal inhibition principle, another anxiety management technique based on the extinction principle has been proposed. This procedure, referred to as reactive inhibition (Malleson, 1959; Yates, 1970) or flooding (Polin, 1959), assumes that repeated presentation of a conditioned (anxiety-evoking) stimulus unaccompanied by reinforcement weakens the conditioned response (anxiety). The effectiveness of prolonged high-intensity stimulation (flooding) over graded exposure in reducing pathological autonomic arousal has been recently demonstrated by Marks, Boulougouris, and Marset (1971) and Watson and Marks (1971). In the reactive inhibition process, the client is instructed to make a deliberate attempt to attend to the anxiety-evoking situation and to all of the accompanying bodily sensations. The rationale is that as long as a person continues to avoid the situation, the anxiety (conditioned) response will persist. In reactive inhibition, the client's cycle of unadaptive anxiety reactions is (theoretically) broken if the client can experience the anxiety without trying to avoid it. As long as the client actively works to maintain the anxiety response, it will be inhibited or weakened and the non-anxious behavior will be reinforced. The first use of this technique was reported by Malleson (1959), who used a hierarchy similar to those used in systematic desensitization. However, in proceeding through the hierarchy, the client was encouraged to feel more frightened rather than relaxed. The results indicated that, after an initial period of distress, the client's level of anxiety completely disappeared.

The reactive inhibition strategy has been tested empirically in several studies in which this process was compared to systematic desensitization based on the reciprocal inhibition principle, explained previously in this chapter. The first study examined the effects of these two procedures on speech anxiety as measured by a self-report speech anxiety form and a manifest anxiety scale. No significant differences among groups were reported on the manifest anxiety scale, but both the reactive and reciprocal inhibition groups reported significantly less anxiety on the speech anxiety form following treatment than did the control group (Calef and MacLean, 1970). However, Blanchard (1971) recommended that, due to the statistical analysis of this study, the results should be interpreted cautiously. Marks, et al. (1971), conducted a study using a crossover design in which half of the phobic subjects received six sessions of flooding followed by six sessions of systematic desensitization, while the other half received the same two treatments in reverse order. Both experimental conditions resulted in improvement on clinical ratings, although flooding achieved significantly better results on some items. A later study compared the effects of reactive inhibition and reciprocal inhibition with a control and placebo discussion group on the level of test anxiety of college freshmen. Subjects' levels of test anxiety decreased significantly in both the reactive and reciprocal inhibition groups following treatment and after eight weeks (Graff, et al., 1971).

The results of the above studies contradict an earlier study conducted by Rachman (1966) in which flooding was used to treat three subjects with a demonstrated aversion to spiders. These subjects were compared to three subjects who had previously undergone desensitization and to three no-treatment control subjects. Results indicated that flooding and control subjects showed no improvement on either a fear thermometer or an avoidance test, while the desensitization subjects improved on both measures. In this study, the subjects who were exposed to flooding were required to imagine extremely frightening scenes in a very short exposure time (two minutes). Wilson (1967) has suggested that the effectiveness of flooding may depend upon the type of responses imagined, while Rachman (1969) and Staub (1968) have stated that a more critical factor may be the exposure time of visualization. Rachman (1969) noted that premature termination of flooding may result in a heightened rather than a reduced level of anxiety.

Morganstern observed that "combining the findings, then, of both human and subhuman research, it seems possible to propose that prolonged exposure (if repeated long enough) may lower physiological arousal to a degree sufficient for subjects to make approach responses (covert or real)." However, Morganstern concluded that because of the contradictory findings and some methodological problems of the research, "it is impossible to conclude any cause-effect relationship between treatment and outcome [1973, p. 331]."

Implosive Therapy

Another anxiety reduction strategy based on extinction principles was introduced as "implosion" by Stampfl and Levis (1967). Levis (1966; 1967) demonstrated that extinction occurred more fully and rapidly when the extinction situation more closely approximated the original learning conditions. Stampfl and Levis (1967) also speculated that greater anxiety reduction occurs as more intense fear is evoked. Implosive therapy is a process involving a reproduction of the "sights, sounds, and factual experiences originally present in the primary conditioning event [Stampfl and Levis, 1968, p. 33]." In implosion therapy, the counselor gives verbal instructions to the client to imagine all of the aversive stimuli *hypothesized* to be present in the original conditioning events (such stimuli include not only the observable symptoms but also associations related to psychoanalytic dynamics of sex, oral functions, aggression, bodily injury, and loss of impulse control). Stampfl and Levis explain the theoretical basis for implosive therapy:

> It is assumed that all aversive cues experienced in imagery function as secondary conditioned stimuli and thus are extinguishable. Exposure to cues representing or approximating these events is likely to elicit relatively high levels of anxiety. Their repetition in the absence of a primary reinforcer, however, should lead to a decrement in their aversiveness through the principle of generalization of extinction and thereby to a reduction in the avoidance reactions which constitute symptomatic behavior [1968, p. 33].

Implosive therapy is a more controversial procedure than flooding, although supposedly extinction processes occur in both techniques. In flooding, intense stimuli are presented for an extended period of time, while in implosion, visualization consists of horrifying and vivid scenes that are assumed to be related to the phobic stimuli. The difference between the two procedures was highlighted by Bandura (1969), who observed, "there is considerable difference between exposing people repeatedly to a fearsome collection of rodents without any adverse effects and depicting them eating human flesh [p. 404]."

Non-experimental case studies have reported successful use of implosion with severely disturbed clients (Stampfl and Levis, 1967; Hogan, 1968; Wolpe, 1969; and Baum and Poser, 1971). However, some unsuccessful attempts have also been reported (Hogan, 1966; Wolpe, 1969), leading Wolpe (1969) to conclude that the results of flooding may depend on individual differences. Experimental studies have been reported with psychotic patients (Hogan, 1966), rat-phobic college females (Kirchner and Hogan, 1966) and snake-phobic subjects (Hogan and Kirchner, 1968). In a critical review of implosive therapy, referring to this series of studies, Morganstern concluded:

> Taken together, the Hogan and Kirchner series offer initially impressive and encouraging findings. On closer inspection, however, it is apparent that the investigations are so replete with methodological deficiencies that it is impossible to draw any firm conclusions about the effectiveness of implosive therapy [1973, pp. 321–322].

Other studies have sought to provide evidence regarding the components of implosive therapy by analyzing different aspects of the treatment package. Kotila (1969) found that a forty-minute continuous implosion group was more successful in reducing snake phobia than either twenty-minute continuous implosion, or distributed implosion for either twenty or forty minutes. Another treatment, called Education Therapy, consisting of giving the subjects information about snakes for six minutes, showed greater fear reduction than any of the implosion therapy methods. Fazio (1970) conducted two experiments of implosion therapy on roach-phobic subjects. When implosion therapy was unsuccessful in fear reduction, Fazio (1970) concluded that discussion was a more important element of improvement. Prochaska (1971) compared the effects of implosive therapy with "symptom cues" versus implosion with "dynamic cues" on test-anxious college students. The symptom-cue group indicated significantly more improvement on an intelligence test, although all imploded subjects reported less anxiety on final exams following treatment and some grade point average increases.

Approximately ten studies have been reported in which implosion therapy has been compared to systematic desensitization. Desensitization was shown to be the superior procedure in four of the studies (Willis and Edwards, 1969; Barrett, 1969; Mealia and Nawas, 1971; Cornish and Dilley, 1973), while the other six studies did not reveal any significant differences between the two treatment procedures (Kirts, 1968; McGlynn, 1968; Carek, 1969; Borkovec, 1970; Horowitz, 1970; and Jacobson, 1970). Morganstern (1973) suggests that the theoretical basis of implosion remains unsupported and that further research is needed before definitive claims can be made regarding the outcomes of implosive therapy.

Steps in Implosion

The procedure of implosive therapy can be summarized in the following steps:

1. An assessment is conducted to determine crucial stimuli associated with the client's anxiety, including symptom cues of situational and environmental stimuli and hypothesized cues involving psychodynamic themes of aggression and sexual material.

2. These cues are arranged on an "Avoidance Serial Cue Hierarchy" (Stampfl and Levis, 1967) with the situational cues on the low end of the hierarchy (presented to the client first) and the hypothesized cues on the higher end of the hierarchy.

3. The client imagines each scene from the hierarchy as verbal instructions are given by the counselor. The client is instructed to "lose" himself/herself and "relive" the scene. A brief example of typical client instructions was given by Hogan:

   . . . An aerophobic would be requested to imagine himself falling off a high building or cliff, or perhaps be instructed to picture himself falling through space and in complete darkness. Ideally, the person should be made aware of his feelings and sensations while falling. Then he should feel the impact of his body with the ground and view his crushed, broken body . . . [1966, p. 26].

4. The counselor attempts to get the client to achieve the highest possible anxiety level with each visualization and when this occurs, the client is held at this level until he "implodes" or spontaneously achieves a reduction in anxiety associated with the particular scene (Stampfl and Levis, 1967).

5. The hierarchy is ascended in this manner until the anxiety elicited by all stimuli is extinguished.

Until more conclusive results of implosion are presented, the counselor should apply the procedure with caution.

Comparison of Anxiety Reduction Strategies

It is apparent that all three of these anxiety reduction strategies (systematic desensitization, flooding, and implosion) are based on differing theoretical principles and processes. Wolpe and Lazarus (1966) predicted that subjects who were presented with anxiety-eliciting stimuli that were too intense (such as in implosion) would become sensitized rather than desensitized to the stimuli, resulting in an increased rather than decreased level of anxiety. In contrast, both flooding and implosion assume that little extinction of conditioned anxiety can occur unless clients experience high levels of intensive emotion to the conditioned stimuli. As Morganstern (1973) indicated, it appears that "the generally accepted theories underlying each technique cannot adequately account for the successes of the other treatment [p. 325]." Comparative studies are recommended to provide data on the theoretical assumptions and the effectiveness of the procedures.

Aversion Therapy

Aversion therapy has been applied most extensively to persistent behaviors potentially harmful to self (often designated as self-injurious) and to others. Bandura (1969) stated that aversion methods ". . . have been applied mainly to persons who wish to gain control over intractable behavior which can produce serious long term consequences for them [p. 501]." Aversion therapy follows the classical conditioning model of learning (discussed in Chapter 1) and involves the systematic pairing of a positively reinforcing (habitual) stimulus (UCS) such as alcohol or fetishes with an aversive stimulus (CS) such as electric shock or drugs so that the habitual stimulus becomes associated with the aversive stimulus.

Bandura (1969) cited three aversive counterconditioning procedures used most often in aversion therapy: electrical stimulation, nauseous pharmacological agents, and symbolically induced aversion. Electrical stimulation has increased in use because it can be used with precise control since shocks can be administered and terminated abruptly and their duration can be varied. Electrical shock has uses to treat fetishes (McGuire and Vallance, 1964), drug addiction (Wolpe, 1965), alcoholism (Hallam, Rachman and Falkowski, 1972), self-destructive behaviors (Rachman and Teasdale, 1969), self-induced seizures (Wright, 1973), and homosexuality (Feldman and MacCulloch, 1965; MacCulloch, Birtles, and Feldman, 1971; Birk, Huddleston, Miller, and Cohler, 1971). A more detailed description of aversion therapy utilizing shock can be found in Feldman and MacCulloch's case report (1965) and in the procedures described by Rachman and Teasdale (1969).

Chemical aversion therapy utilizes pharmacological agents as the aversive stimuli that are contiguously paired with the self-destructive and/or undesirable behavior. Most of these pharmacological agents are aversive in that they produce a noxious or nauseous odor. These procedures, as well as several of the requirements for successful counterconditioning, are presented in a case reporting the use of chemical aversion therapy with a male transvestite who was concerned about the legal and personal consequences of his behavior (Lavin, Thorpe, Barker, Blakemore, and Conway, 1961). Another successful case using chemical aversion therapy was reported in Raymond's (1965) treatment of a fetishistic client. Rachman and Teasdale (1969) discussed applications of this procedure with alcoholics.

The third procedure, which may have less side effects and be more desirable to some clients, is symbolically induced aversion therapy. In this procedure, the client imagines a repulsive experience during the problem, which also may be actually or symbolically presented. As an example, to reduce alcohol drinking when a variety of alcoholic beverages and odor are introduced, the client imagines repulsive experiences resulting from drinking, such as nausea, hangover, etc. As with chemical and electrical aversion therapy, the conditioning trials are repeated until the formerly positive stimuli alone elicit feelings of repulsion. Several descriptions of "successful" symbolic aversion therapy in treating homosexuals (Miller, 1963) and alcoholics (Abrams, 1964; Anant, 1967) have been reported.

A variation of these three aversion therapy procedures was recently reported by Schmahl, Lichtenstein, and Harris (1972). Habituated smokers received either warm, smoky air or warm, mentholated air as the aversive stimulus paired with smoking behavior. After eight sessions, at termination, all twenty-eight subjects abstained from cigarette smoking. After six months, sixteen had remained abstinent from further cigarette smoking.

Bandura (1969) declared that "the major value of aversive procedures is that they provide a rapid means of achieving control over injurious behavior for a period during which alternative, and more rewarding, modes of behavior can be established [p. 554]." However, the application of aversive procedures is complicated and failure to apply a procedural variable correctly can result in harmful effects. Those using these techniques should be thoroughly aware of all procedural variables as well as the advantages and limitations of the procedures and corresponding ethical considerations. Ethical considerations suggest that the counselor is responsible for providing the client with accurate information about all treatment alternatives and possible outcomes. The client is ultimately responsible for deciding upon the type of procedure to be used and potential goals for the treatment (Bandura, 1969). Furthermore, self-control procedures for managing the undesired behavior should be included with the aversion therapy treatment.

Applications of Behavioral Strategies for Groups

Various behavioral models of groups have been proposed in the last several years (Varenhorst, 1969; Liberman, 1970a and b; Thoresen, 1971; Lawrence and Sundel, 1972; Staub, 1972; Dustin and George, 1973; Krumboltz and Potter, 1973; and Rose, 1973). All of these frameworks emphasize clearly stated behavioral objectives for each group member and the possible application of all of the intervention strategies presented in this chapter and in others, including social modeling, social reinforcement, systematic desensitization, assertive training, and behavior rehearsal. An advantage of a small group setting can be the opportunity for systematic application of learning principles designed to assist members in reaching their goals in an efficient and effective manner. Dustin and George (1973) observed that the processes of learning and relearning of behaviors and attitudes may be greatly facilitated in a group setting, since group members may be potential social models and can provide multiple sources of reinforcement.

Thoresen (1971) suggested that conceptualizing the group process in a behavioral framework can make group counseling accountable by demonstrating that specific changes in individual members do occur as a result of the group experience. While group processes and procedures have traditionally been labeled in vague terms, a recent trend has enabled further specification of the behaviors that can be exhibited by both leaders and members. Processes that have been previously described as leading to trust and openness have been well defined by Krumboltz and Potter (1973), who presented a very specific delineation of group behaviors that can result in such outcomes. These authors also suggested specific leader behaviors and group exercises designed to facilitate overall group goals.

There seems to be agreement regarding the purposes of behavioral processes for the group members. Thoresen (1971) and Dustin and George (1973) observed that groups can assist clients who demonstrate deficient decision-making skills, ineffective academic skills, inappropriate social skills, and excessive fears and anxieties. Rose (1973) suggested that the problems of group members that can be treated within a group setting fall into one of five categories: adaptive behaviors that generally need to be increased, maladaptive behaviors that generally need to be decreased, behaviors that are adaptive under some conditions but not others, problems maintained by inadequate or inappropriate reinforcers, and environmental problems.

The proponents of a behavioral group model generally agree that a group setting can provide a somewhat unique atmosphere for individual members to accomplish their own personal goals. All of the authors noted that the client is presented with a wider range of relationships in a group setting than in a dyadic relationship. This not only gives the client an opportunity to perform leadership and/or teaching roles for other persons (Rose, 1973), but also maximizes the opportunity for social reinforcement and provides for a variety of potential social models. Dustin and George (1973) noted that "group discussions can strengthen discrimination learning as members come to compare effective behavior with behavior that does not achieve desired goals [p. 193]."

Liberman (1970a and b) has suggested that more long-term learning could result from a group experience if 1) goals for each member were cearly specified in behavioral terms, 2) both the group leader(s) and the members identified ways to monitor progress toward goals, and 3) the leader(s) applied basic learning principles of modeling, shaping, and positive reinforcement in a systematic manner within the group. All of the proposed models emphasized the importance of assessing the member's problem, selecting problems to work on in the group, defining behavioral goals, and monitoring progress toward the ultimate goal. Lawrence and Sundel (1972) observed that the success of any group may be determined by the degree to which each member's specified goal is attained. Several authors have advocated using a contract between the member and the group leader (Lawrence and Sundel, 1972; Rose, 1973; Dustin and George, 1973). Terms of the contract typically include such group ground rules as attendance at group sessions, working on designated problems and goals, and completing tasks between group sessions.

In order for the members to achieve designated goals, specific procedures can be applied within the group setting. New behaviors can be developed through social and self modeling, learning by observation or imitation of others engaged in desired behaviors, or by viewing oneself (usually through video feedback) demonstrate appropriate behaviors (Creer and Miklich, 1970). Desired models can be provided more easily in a heterogeneous group comprised both of members who possess specific behaviors in their repertoire and of members who display certain behavioral deficits. The possibilities of acquiring new behaviors in groups through social modeling procedures has been documented by Krumboltz and Thoresen (1964).

New behaviors can be strengthened through shaping or successive approximation, positive reinforcement, and rehearsal. Usually a member can attain a terminal goal more easily when the goal is sub-divided into small increments, sub-steps, or intermediate goals as described in Chapter 2. As Liberman (1972) has stated, common group behavior too often involves confrontation of a member's ineffective behavior. While the confrontation may seem like punishment, it may often serve to reinforce the inappropriate behavior by increasing the amount of attention focused on the member. Liberman (1972) suggests that observing and reinforcing small steps of behavior change which resemble the overall goal may be a more effective group behavior than confrontation. Positive reinforcement can occur in massive quantities in a group setting and can be used to develop new behaviors and to strengthen existing behaviors that an individual may desire to increase (Asch, 1956; Shapiro and Birk, 1967; and Staub, 1972). Multiple sources of feedback can also provide reinforcement, since knowledge of one's performance may be a potentially important reinforcer of learning. Additionally, behavior can be strengthened through self-reinforcement by determining those conditions under which the individual can reward himself or herself for desired responses.

Rehearsal, or the opportunity to experiment and practice desired behaviors, is another valuable procedure in a group setting. Rehearsal can be used in acquisition of a variety of group goals, including reducing fear responses through sequenced imagery, providing correct reinforcement for other behaviors (Cautela, 1970), and acquiring new behaviors in a relatively anxiety-free situation. In the latter case, variations of the behavior rehearsal procedure described earlier in this chapter, include the "fixed role" exercise, the "role reversal" strategy and the "role instruction" procedure. In the "fixed role" procedure (Kelly, 1955) the client is instructed to "try on" the desired behaviors, or behave "as if" he/she were demonstrating the behaviors he/she would like to achieve. Rose (1973) defined fixed role therapy as "a form of behavior rehearsal followed by a behavioral assignment to continue the rehearsal in the real world [p. 127]." The "role reversal" procedure involves two or more members of the group taking opposite roles. For example, one member may take the role of his parent while the other member takes the role of the son. Or, all the males in the group can take the part of females, while the females take the role of males. This procedure allows a client not only to demonstrate desired behaviors, but also to anticipate and respond to potential consequences of his/her newly acquired behaviors. The "role instruction" (Rose, 1973) procedure gives specific instructions to one member about the behaviors he/she rehearses within the group during the ongoing group interaction while the group continues to handle other problems and tasks. For example, a member who desires to make less frequent critical remarks may be instructed to practice positive verbal statements to other group members during the ongoing group sessions.

Behavior rehearsal and its variations can be most effective in a group setting when clear-cut objectives and tasks have been identified. The element of practice may be even more powerful when the leader models the behavior and when the group members are encouraged to praise the target behaviors being demonstrated (Liberman, 1972). As Houts and Serber (1972) have stressed, having a "turn on" in a group experience "does not depend on extravagant and unrealistic expectations of participants [p. 13]." Groups whose sole aim is simply to provide a "here and now" experience will simply remain a "turn on." But, groups that do not specify goals and evaluate outcomes will remain "irrelevant for those who lack skills for meeting the demands of life . . . and the many people who need to *learn* more effective ways to express themselves and to deal with their feelings," and with other persons (Houts and Serber, 1972, p. 15).

Concluding Comments

The various procedures described in this monograph may point to considerable heterogeneity present within a behavioral counseling framework. Behavioral counseling cannot be justifiably described as an "all-purpose, single method" therapy (Bandura, 1969, p. 89). The behavioral counselor will select different procedures to use with a client, depending on the nature of the problem. Since the particular counseling strategy employed is adapted for the individual client, accurate problem identification is a critical variable in the effectiveness of the therapeutic procedure. As Lazarus observes, "faulty problem identification (inadequate assessment) is probably the greatest impediment to successful therapy [1974, p. 684]."

The procedures described in the monograph are based upon results of case studies and empirical research. The research studies provide data about the potential effectiveness of a particular therapeutic procedure. However, the results should be interpreted cautiously. Generalizations about therapeutic procedures can be misleading — what works with one client or situation may not have the same effect with another client or situation. Behavioral counseling research supports the idea that therapeutic procedures "are not universal panaceas, indiscriminately effective under all circumstances [Heller, 1969]."

This monograph has summarized initial procedures in behavioral counseling and some procedures based on social modeling and classical learning. Although some overlap may exist, procedures based on operant learning are presented in a second monograph by the authors: *Behavioral Counseling: Operant Procedures, Self-Management Strategies, and Recent Innovations* (Cormier and Cormier, 1975), which monograph also describes some of the innovative behavioral counseling methods that have emerged within the last decade and some possible future trends.

APPENDIX

Partial List of Publications

*The Center for Behavior Therapy
News Brief*
The Center for Behavior Therapy
8712 Wilshire Boulevard
Beverly Hills, California 90211

Behavior Modification Monographs
Roger E. Ulrich, Editor
Department of Psychology
Western Michigan University
Kalamazoo, Michigan 49001

Speaking of Behaviorists
P. O. Box 171
Centerville Branc
Dayton, Ohio 45459

PSI Newsletter
Department of Psychology
Georgetown University
Washington, D.C. 20007

The Boulder Behaviorist
Boulder River School and Hospital
Boulder, Montana 59632

*School Applications of Learning
Technology*
Robert P. Hawkins, Editor
Department of Psychology
Western Michigan University
Kalamazoo, Michigan 49001

*Classroom Applications of
Reinforcement Theory (CART)*
Michael L. Boyle, Editor
Department of Psychological
Services
John Archer School
Belair, Maryland 21014

*Bulletin de l'Association pour
l'Analyse et la Modification du
Comportement*

Gilles Trudel and Jean-Marie
Boisvert, Editors
Hôspital Saint-Jean-de-Dieu
Montréal, Gameline
Québec

*Teachers Experimental Analysis of
Motivation (TEAM)*
Manuel L. Morales, Editor
Anne Arundel County Learning
Center
Adams Park, Clay Street
Annapolis, Maryland 21401

Be-Mod
Stuart Silverman, Editor
10004 Oak Hill Drive
Temple Terrace, Florida 33617

The Learning Analyst Newsletter
G. Roy Mayer, Editor
Department of Guidance and Pupil
Personnel Services
California State University, Los
Angeles
5151 State University Drive
Los Angeles, California 90032

*Research and Application of
Techniques in Education (RATE)*
Rose Hesse, Editor
Special Student Services
Clark County School District
2832 East Flamingo Road
Las Vegas, Nevada 89109

*Bulletin of Behavior Modification
in Mental Retardation*
David W. Smith, Editor
Greene Valley Developmental
Center
P. O. Box 3087
Greeneville, Tennessee 37743

BIBLIOGRAPHY

Abrams, S. An evaluation of hypothesis in the treatment of alcoholics. *American Journal of Psychiatry*, 1964, *120*, 1160–1165.

Alberti, R. E., & Emmons, M. L. *Your perfect right*. St. Louis Obispo, California: Impact, 1970.

Allen, G. J. Effectiveness of study counseling and desensitization in alleviating test anxiety in college students. *Journal of Abnormal Psychology*, 1971, 77, 282–289.

Anant, S. S. A note on the treatment of alcoholics by the verbal aversion technique. *Canadian Psychologist*, 1967, *8*, 19–22.

Asch, S. E. Studies of independence and conformity. A minority of one against a unanimous majority. *Psychological Monographs*, 1956, *70* (Whole No. 416).

Atkinson, D. R. Effect of selected behavior modification techniques on student-initiated action. *Journal of Counseling Psychology*, 1971, *18*, 395–400.

Auerswald, M. C. Differential reinforcing power of restatement and interpretation of client production of affect. *Journal of Counseling Psychology*, 1974, *21*, 9–14.

Azrin, N. H., Holz, W., Ulrich, R., & Goldiamond, I. The control of the content of conversation through reinforcement. *Journal of the Experimental Analysis of Behavior*, 1961, *4*, 25–30.

Bandura, A. Psychotherapy as a learning process. *Psychological Bulletin*, 1961, *58*, 143–159.

Bandura, A. Influences of model's reinforcement contingencies on the acquisition of imitative responses. *Journal of Personality and Social Psychology*, 1965, *1*, 589–595.

Bandura, A. *Principles of behavior modification*. New York: Holt, Rinehart and Winston, 1969.

Bandura, A. Behavior theory and the models of man. *American Psychologist*, 1974, *29*, 859–869.

Bandura, A., Ross, D., & Ross, S. A. Vicarious reinforcement and imitative learning. *Journal of Abnormal and Social Psychology*, 1963, *67*, 601–607.

Bandura, A., & Walters, A. H. *Social learning and personality development*. New York: Holt, Rinehart and Winston, 1963.

Bandura, A., & Mischel, W. The influence of models in modifying delay of gratification patterns. *Journal of Personality and Social Psychology,* 1965, *2,* 698–705.

Bandura, A., Blanchard, E. D., & Ritter, B. J. The relative efficacy of desensitization and modeling approaches for inducing behavioral, affective and attitudinal change. Unpublished, Stanford, California: Stanford University, 1969.

Barabasz, A. F. Group desensitization of test anxiety in elementary school. Paper presented at American Educational Research Association, Chicago, Illinois, 1972.

Barnabei, F., Cormier, W. H., & Nye, L. S. Determining the effects of three counselor verbal responses on client verbal behavior. *Journal of Counseling Psychology,* 1974, *21,* 355–359.

Barrett, C. L. Systematic desensitization versus implosive therapy. *Journal of Abnormal Psychology,* 1969, *74,* 587–592.

Baum, M., & Poser, E. G. Comparison of flooding procedures in animals and man. *Behaviour Research and Therapy,* 1971, *9,* 249–254.

Bentler, P. M. An infant's phobia treated with reciprocal inhibition therapy. *Journal of Child Psychology and Psychiatry,* 1962, *3,* 185–189.

Berwick, P., & O'Zeil, L. J. The use of meditation as a behavioral technique. *Behavior Therapy,* 1973, *4,* 743–745.

Bijou, S. W., Peterson, R. F., & Ault, M. H. A method to integrate descriptive and experimental field studies at the level of data and empirical concepts. *Journal of Applied Behavior Analysis,* 1968, *1,* 175–191.

Bijou, S. W., Peterson, R. F., Harris, F. R., Allen, K. E., & Johnston, M. S. Methodology for experimental studies of young children in natural settings. *The Psychological Record,* 1969, *19,* 177–210.

Birk, L., Huddleston, W., Miller, E., & Cohler, B. Avoidance conditioning for homosexuality. *Archives of General Psychology,* 1971, *25,* 314–325.

Blanchard, E. B. A comparison of reciprocal inhibition and reactive inhibition therapies in the treatment of speech anxiety: A methodological critique. *Behavior Therapy,* 1971, *2,* 103–106.

Bloomfield, H. H. Assertive training in an outpatient group of chronic schizophrenics: A preliminary report. *Behavior Therapy,* 1973, *4,* 277–281.

Bond, I. K., & Hutchinson, H. C. Application of reciprocal inhibition therapy to exhibitionism. *Canadian Medical Association Journal,* 1960, *83,* 23–25.

Borkovec, T. D. The comparative effectiveness of systematic desensitization and implosion therapy and the effect of expectancy manipulation on the elimination of fear. Unpublished doctoral dissertation, University of Illinois, 1970.

Calef, R. A., & MacLean, G. D. A comparison of reciprocal inhibition and reactive inhibition therapies in the treatment of speech anxiety. *Behavior Therapy,* 1970, *1,* 51–58.

Campbell, D. T., & Stanley, J. C. *Experimental and quasi-experimental designs for research.* Chicago: Rand McNally, 1966.

Carek, R. G. A comparison of two behavioral therapy techniques in the treatment of rat "phobias." Unpublished doctoral dissertation, University of Iowa, 1969.

Carkhuff, R. R. *Helping and human relations: A primer for lay and professional helpers.* Vol. 2. *Practice and Research.* New York: Holt, Rinehart and Winston, 1969.

Cautela, J. R. Covert reinforcement. *Behavior Therapy,* 1970, *1,* 33–50.

Cautela, J. R., and Kastenbaum, R. A reinforcement survey schedule for use in therapy, training, and research. *Psychological Reports,* 1967, *20,* 1115–1130.

Clopton, J., & Risbrough, R. Sexual arousal for desensitization. *Behavior Therapy,* 1973, 5, 741–742.

Cormier, L. S. & Cormier, W. H. *Behavioral Counseling: Operant procedures, self-management strategies, and recent innovations.* Boston: Houghton Mifflin, 1975.

Cormier, W. H. & Nye, L. S. Discrimination model for systematic counselor training. Paper presented at the annual meeting of the American Educational Research Association, New Orleans, Louisiana, 1973.

Cormier, W. H. & Cormier, L. S. Problem identification in counseling. Unpublished learning module, West Virginia University, 1974a.

Cormier, W. H. & Cormier, L. S. Establishing goals in counseling. Unpublished learning module, West Virginia University, Morgantown, West Virginia, 1974b.

Cormier, W. H. & Cormier, L. S. Developing and implementing self-instructional modules for counselor training. Unpublished, West Virginia University, Morgantown, West Virginia, 1974c.

Cormier, W. H. & Cormier, L. S. Behavior rehearsal. Videotaped module, West Virginia University, Morgantown, West Virginia, 1974d.

Cormier, W. H. & Cormier, L. S. Assertive training. Unpublished learning module, West Virginia University, Morgantown, West Virginia, 1974e.

Cornish, R. D., & Dilley, J. S. Comparison of three methods of reducing test anxiety: Systematic desensitization, implosive therapy, and study counseling. *Journal of Counseling Psychology,* 1973, *20,* 499–503.

Creer, T. L., & Miklich, D. R. The application of a self-modeling procedure to modify inappropriate behavior: A preliminary report. *Behaviour Research and Therapy,* 1970, 8, 91–92.

Crowley, T. The conditionability of positive and negative self-reference emotional affect statements in a counseling type interview. Unpublished doctoral dissertation, University of Massachusetts, Amherst, 1970.

Davison, G. C. The influence of systematic desensitization, relaxation, and graded exposure to imagined aversive stimuli on the modification of phobic behavior. Unpublished doctoral dissertation, Stanford University, 1965.

Dawley, H. H., & Wenrich, W. W. *Patient's manual for systematic desensitization.* Palo Alto, California: Veteran's Workshop, 1973.

Deffenbacher, J. L., & Kemper, C. C. Systematic desensitization of test anxiety in junior high students. *The School Counselor,* 1974, *22,* 216–224.

Dengrove, E. Treatment of non-phobic disorders by the behavioral therapies. Lecture to the Association for Advancement of Behavioral Therapies, New York, December, 1966.

Dollard, J., & Miller, N. E. *Personality and psychotherapy.* New York: McGraw-Hill, 1950.

Donner, L., & Guerney, B., Jr. Automated group desensitization for test anxiety. *Behaviour Research and Therapy,* 1969, *7,* 1–14.

Dua, P. S. Group desensitization of a phobia with three massing procedures. *Journal of Counseling Psychology,* 1972, *19,* 125–129.

Dustin, R., & George, R. *Action counseling for behavior change.* New York: Intext Press, 1973.

Eisenberg, S., & Delaney, L. Using video simulation of counseling for training counselors. *Journal of Counseling Psychology,* 1970, *17,* 15–19.

Emery, J. R., & Krumboltz, J. D. Standard versus individualized hierarchies in desensitization to reduce test anxiety. *Journal of Counseling Psychology,* 1967, *14,* 204–209.

Eysenck, H. J. (Ed.). *Behavior therapy and the neuroses.* New York: Pergamon Press, 1960.

Fazio, A. F. Treatment components in implosive therapy. *Journal of Abnormal Psychology,* 1970, *76,* 211–219.

Feldman, M. P., & MacCulloch, M. J. The application of anticipatory avoidance learning to the treatment of homosexuality: Theory, technique and preliminary results. *Behaviour Research and Therapy,* 1965, *2,* 165–183.

Frankel, M. Effects of videotape modeling and self-confrontation techniques on microcounseling behavior. *Journal of Counseling Psychology.* 1971. *18,* 465–471.

Franks, C. M. Comment to Lang, P. J. Stimulus control, response control, and the desensitization of fear. In *Learning approaches to therapeutic behavior change.* Chicago: Aldine Press, 1970, pp. 174–181.

Franks, C. M., & Brady, J. P. What is behavior therapy and why a new journal? *Behavior Therapy,* 1970, *1,* 1–3.

Franks, C. M., & Wilson, G. T. (Eds.). *Annual review of behavior therapy.* New York: Brunner/Mazel Publishers, 1973.

Fretz, B. R. Postural movements in a counseling dyad. *Journal of Counseling Psychology,* 1966, *13,* 335–343.

Fry, (Dua), P. S. Effects of desensitization treatment on core-condition training. *Journal of Counseling Psychology,* 1973, *20,* 214–219.

Galassi, J. P., Delo, J. S., Galassi, M. D., & Bastien, S. The college self-expression scale: A measure of assertiveness. *Behavior Therapy*, 1974, *5*, 165–171.

Galassi, J. P., Galassi, M. D. & Litz, M. C. Assertive training in groups using video feedback. *Journal of Counseling Psychology*, 1974, *21*, 390–394.

Garvey, W. P., & Hegrenes, J. R. Desensitization techniques in the treatment of school phobia. *American Journal of Orthopsychiatry*, 1966, *36*, 147–152.

Geer, J. H. The development of a scale to measure fear. *Behaviour Research and Therapy*, 1965, *3*, 45–53.

Gelder, M. G., & Marks, I. M. Severe agoraphobia: A controlled prospective trial of behavioral therapy. *British Journal of Psychiatry*, 1966, *112*, 309–319.

Glass, G. V., Willson, V. L., & Gottman, J. M. *Design and Analysis of Time-Series Experiments*. Boulder, Colorado: Laboratory of Education Research, University of Colorado, 1972.

Goldberg, J., & D'Zurilla, T. Demonstration of slide projection as an alternative to imagined stimulus presentation in systematic desensitization. *Psychological Reports*, 1968, *23*, 527–533.

Goldstein, A., Serber, M., & Piaget, G. W. Induced anger as a reciprocal inhibitor of fear. *Journal of Behavior Therapy and Experimental Psychiatry*, 1970, *7*, 67–70.

Goldstein, A. P., Martens, J., Hubben, J., van Belle, H. A., Schaaf, W., Wiersma, H., & Goedhart, A. The use of modeling to increase independent behavior. *Behaviour Research and Therapy*, 1973, *11*, 31–42.

Graff, R., MacLean, G., & Loving, A. Group reactive inhibition and reciprocal inhibition therapies with anxious college students. *Journal of Counseling Psychology*, 1971, *18*, 431–436.

Green, A. H., & Marlatt, G. A. Effects of instructions and modeling upon affective and descriptive verbalization. *Journal of Abnormal Psychology*, 1972, *80*, 189–196.

Greenspoon, J. The reinforcing effect of two spoken sounds on the frequency of two responses. *American Journal of Psychology*, 1955, *68*, 409–416.

Haase, R. F. The relationship of sex and instructional set to the relation of interpersonal interaction distance in a counseling analogue. *Journal of Counseling Psychology*, 1970, *17*, 233–236.

Haase, R. F., & Tepper, D. T., Jr. Nonverbal components of empathic communication. *Journal of Counseling Psychology*, 1972, *19*, 417–424.

Hackney, H. L. Construct reduction of counselor empathy and positive regard: A replication and extension. Unpublished doctoral dissertation, University of Massachusetts, 1970.

Hackney, H. L., & Nye, L. S. *Counseling strategies and objectives.* Englewood Cliffs, New Jersey: Prentice-Hall, 1973.

Hackstian, A. L., Zimmer, J. M., & Newby, J. F. A descriptive and comparative study of the dimensions of counselee response. Technical Reports, University of Massachusetts, School of Education, January, 1971, No. 11.

Hallam, R., Rachman, S., & Falkowski, W. Subjective, attitudinal and physiological effects of electrical aversion therapy. *Behaviour Research and Therapy*, 1972, *10*, 1–13.

Hekmat, H. The role of imagination in semantic desensitization. *Behavior Therapy*, 1972, 3, 223–231.

Heller, K. Effects of modeling procedures in helping relationships. *Journal of Consulting and Clinical Psychology*, 1969, 33, 522–526.

Hersen, M., Eisler, R. & Miller, P. Development of assertive responses: Clinical, measurement and research considerations. *Behaviour Research and Therapy*, 1973, *11*, 505–521.

Hilgard, E. R., & Bower, G. H. *Theories of learning* (3rd ed.). New York: Appleton-Century-Crofts, 1966.

Hogan, R. A. Implosive therapy in the short term treatment of psychotics. *Psychotherapy: Theory Research and Practice*, 1966, 3, 25–31.

Hogan, R. A. The implosive technique. *Behaviour Research and Therapy*, 1968, 6, 423–431.

Hogan, R. A., & Kirchner, J. H. Implosive, eclectic verbal and bibliotherapy in the treatment of fears of snakes. *Behaviour Research and Therapy*, 1968, 6, 167–171.

Holz, W. C., & Azrin, N. H. Conditioning human verbal behavior. In W. K. Honig (Ed.), *Operant behavior: Areas of research and application*. New York: Appleton-Century-Crofts, 1966, pp. 790–826.

Horowitz, S. L. Strategies within hypnosis for reducing phobic behavior. *Journal of Abnormal Psychology*, 1970, 75, 104–112.

Hosford, R. E. Overcoming fear of speaking in a group. In J. D. Krumboltz and C. E. Thoresen, *Behavioral counseling: Cases and techniques*, New York: Holt, Rinehart and Winston, 1969a, pp. 80–82.

Hosford, R. E. Behavioral counseling — A contemporary overview. *The Counseling Psychologist*, 1969b, 7, 1–32.

Hosford, R. E. Personal communication, 1972.

Hosford, R. E., & DeVisser, H. Ethnic variable in social modeling. Unpublished manuscript, University of California, Santa Barbara, 1972.

Houts, P. S., & Serber, M. (Eds.). *After the turn on, what?* Champaign, Illinois: Research Press, 1972.

Huck, S. W., Cormier, W. H., & Bounds, W. G. *Reading statistics and research*. New York: Harper and Row, 1974.

Ivey, A. *Microcounseling: Innovations in interviewing training*. Springfield, Illinois: C. C. Thomas, 1971.

Jacobson, E. *Progressive relaxation*. Chicago: University of Chicago Press, 1938.

Jacobson, H. A. Reciprocal inhibition and implosive therapy: A comparative study of a fear of snakes. Unpublished doctoral dissertation, Memphis State University, 1970.

Janis, I., & Mann, L. Effectiveness of emotional role playing in modifying smoking habits and attitudes. *Journal of Experimental Research in Personality*, 1965, *7*, 17–27.

Jones, M. C. A laboratory study of fear: The case of Peter. *Pedagogical Seminar*, 1924a, *31*, 308–315.

Jones, M. C. The elimination of children's fears. *Journal of Experimental Psychology*, 1924b, *7*, 383–390.

Kanfer, F. H., & Marston, A. R. Human reinforcement: Vicarious and direct. *Journal of Experimental Psychology*, 1963, *65*, 292–296.

Kanfer, F. H., & Phillips, J. S. *Learning foundations of behavior therapy.* New York: Wiley and Sons, 1970.

Kelly, G. A. *The psychology of personal constructions.* 2 volumes. New York: Norton, 1955.

Kennedy, J. J., & Zimmer, J. M. Reinforcing value of five stimulus conditions in a quasi-counseling situation. *Journal of Counseling Psychology*, 1968, *15*, 357–362.

Kirchner, J. H., & Hogan, R. A. The therapist variable in the implosion of phobias. *Psychotherapy: Theory, Research, and Practice*, 1966, *3*, 102–104.

Kirts, S. M. C. An experimental analogue comparing two models of psychotherapy: Reciprocal inhibitions and implosive therapy. Unpublished doctoral dissertation, University of Southern California, 1968.

Kotila, R. R. The effects of education and four varieties of impressive therapy on fear of snakes. Unpublished doctoral dissertation, University of Wisconsin, 1969.

Krasner, L., & Ullmann, L. P. (Eds.). *Research in behavior modification.* New York: Holt, Rinehart and Winston, 1965.

Krumboltz, J. D. Behavioral goals for counseling. *Journal of Counseling Psychology*, 1966a, *13*, 153–159.

Krumboltz, J. D. (Ed.). *Revolution in counseling.* Boston: Houghton Mifflin, 1966b.

Krumboltz, J. D., & Thoresen, C. E. The effects of behavioral counseling in groups and individual settings on information-seeking behavior. *Journal of Counseling Psychology*, 1964, *11*, 324–333.

Krumboltz, J. D., & Schroeder, W. W. Promoting career planning through reinforcement. *The Personnel and Guidance Journal*, 1965, *44*, 19–26.

Krumboltz, J. D., Varenhorst, B. B., & Thoresen, C. E. Nonverbal factors in the effectiveness of models in counseling. *Journal of Counseling Psychology*, 1967, *14*, 412–418.

Krumboltz, J. D., & Thoresen, C. E. (Eds.). *Behavioral counseling: Cases and techniques.* New York: Holt, Rinehart and Winston, 1969.

Krumboltz, J. D., & Potter, B. Behavioral techniques for developing trust, cohesiveness, and goal accomplishment. *Educational Technology*, 1973, *12*, 26–30.

Krumboltz, J. D., & Thoresen, C. E. (Eds.). *Behavioral counseling methods*. New York: Holt, Rinehart and Winston (In press).

LaFleur, N. K., & Johnson, R. G. Separate effects of social modeling and reinforcement in counseling adolescents. *Journal of Counseling Psychology*, 1972, *19*, 292–295.

Lang, P., & Lazovik, A. Systematic desensitization psychotherapy: Experimental analogue. Manual of procedure mimeograph, 1960.

Lang, P., & Lazovik, A. Experimental desensitization of a phobia. *Journal of Abnormal Psychology*, 1963, *66*, 519–525.

Lavin, N. I., Thorpe, J. G., Barker, J. C., Blakemore, C. B., & Conway, C. G. Behavior therapy in a case of transvestism. *Journal of Nervous and Mental Disorders*, 1961, *133*, 346–353.

Lawrence, H., & Sundel, M. Behavior modification in adult groups. *Social Work*, 1972, *17*, 34–43.

Lazarus, A. A. New methods in psychotherapy: A case study. *South African Medical Journal*, 1958, *32*, 660–664.

Lazarus, A. A. Group therapy of phobic disorders by systematic desensitization. *Journal of Abnormal and Social Psychology*, 1961, *63*, 504–510.

Lazarus, A. A. Behavior rehearsal vs. non-directive therapy vs. advice in effecting behavior change. *Behaviour Research and Therapy*, 1966, *4*, 209–212.

Lazarus, A. A. In support of technical electicism. *Psychological Reports*, 1967, *21*, 415–416.

Lazarus, A. A. *Behavior therapy and beyond*. New York: McGraw-Hill, 1971.

Lazarus, A. A. Multimodal behavior therapy: Treating the "basic id". In C. M. Franks & G. T. Wilson (Eds.), *Annual review of behavior therapy: Theory and practice: II*. New York: Brunner/Mazel, 1974, pp. 679–690.

Lazarus, A. A., & Rachman, S. The use of systematic desensitization in psychotherapy. *South African Medical Journal*, 1957, *32*, 934–937.

Lazarus, A. A., & Abramovitz, A. The use of emotive imagery in the treatment of children's phobias. *Journal of Mental Science*, 1962, *108*, 191.

Levis, D. G. Effects of serial CS presentation and other characteristics of the CS on the conditioned avoidance response. *Psychological Reports*, 1966, *3*, 102–104.

Levis, D. J. Implosive therapy, part II: The subhuman analogue, the strategy, and the techniques. In S. G. Armitage (Ed.), *Behavior modification techniques in the treatment of emotional disorders*. Battle Creek, Michigan: V. A. Publications, 1967.

Liberman, R. A behavioral approach to group dynamics. I. Reinforcement and prompting of cohesiveness in group therapy. *Behavior Therapy*, 1970a, *2*, 141–175.

Liberman, R. A behavioral approach to group dynamics. II. Reinforcing and prompting hostility-to-the-therapist in group therapy. *Behavior Therapy*, 1970b, *3*, 312–327.

Liberman, R. Learning interpersonal skills in groups: Harnessing the behavioristic horse to the humanistic wagon. In P. S. Houts and M. Serber, *After the turn on, what?* Champaign, Illinois: Research Press Co., 1972, pp. 89–108.

Lindsley, O. R. Operant conditioning methods applied to research in chronic schizophrenia. *Psychiatric Research Reports*, 1956, *5*, 118–138.

Loeffler, D. Counseling and the psychology of communication. *The Personnel and Guidance Journal*, 1970, *48*, 629–636.

Lomont, J. F. Reciprocal inhibition or extinction? *Behaviour Research and Therapy*, 1965, *3*, 209–219.

Lomont, J. R., Gilner, F. H., Spector, N. J., & Skinner, K. K. Group assertion training and group insight therapies. *Psychological Reports*, 1969, *25*, 463–470.

London, P. The end of ideology in behavior modification. *American Psychologist*, 1972, *27*, 913–926.

Lovaas, O. I. A behavior therapy approach to the treatment of childhood schizophrenia. In J. P. Hill (Ed.), *Minnesota symposia on child psychology*. Vol. 1. Minneapolis: University of Minnesota Press, 1967, pp. 108–159.

Lovaas, O. I., Koegel, R., Simmons, J. Q., & Long, J. S. Some generalization and follow-up measures on autistic children in behavior therapy. *Journal of Applied Behavior Analysis*, 1973, *6*, 131–166.

Luthe, W. Autogenic training: Method, research, and application in medicine. In C. T. Tart (Ed.), *Altered states of consciousness*. New York: John Wiley and Sons, 1969, pp. 309–319.

MacCulloch, M. J., Birtles, C. J., & Feldman, M. P. Anticipatory avoidance learning for the treatment of homosexuality: Recent developments in an automatic aversion therapy system. *Behavior Therapy*, 1971, *2*, 151–169.

McFall, R. M., & Marston, A. R. An experimental investigation of behavior rehearsal in assertive training. *Journal of Abnormal Psychology*, 1970, *76*, 295–303.

McFall, R. M., & Lillesand, D. B. Behavior rehearsal with modeling and coaching in assertion training. *Journal of Abnormal Psychology*, 1971, *77*, 313–323.

McFall, R. M., & Twentyman, C. T. Four experiments on the relative contributions of rehearsal, modeling, and coaching to assertion training. *Journal of Abnormal Psychology*, 1973, *81*, 199–218.

McGlynn, F. D. Systematic desensitization, implosive therapy and the aversiveness of imaginal hierarchy items. Unpublished doctoral dissertation, University of Missouri, 1968.

McGlynn, F., Wilson, A., & Linder, L. Systematic desensitization of snake-avoidance with individualized and non-individualized hierarchies. *Journal of Behavior Therapy and Experimental Psychiatry*, 1970, 7, 201–204.

McGuire, R. J., & Vallance, M. Aversion therapy by electric shock: A simple technique. *British Medical Journal*, 1964, *1*, 151–153.

Madsen, C., & Ullmann, L. Innovations in the desensitization of frigidity. *Behaviour Research and Therapy*, 1967, 5, 67–68.

Mager, R. F. *Preparing instructional objectives*. Belmont, California: Fearon Publishers, 1962.

Mahoney, M. J., & Thoresen, C. E. (Eds.). *Self-control: Power to the person*. Monterey, California: Brooks/Cole, 1974.

Malleson, N. Panic and phobia. *Lancet*, 1959, 7, 225–227.

Mann, J. Vicarious desensitization of test anxiety through observation of a video-taped treatment. *Journal of Counseling Psychology*, 1972, *19*, 1–7.

Mann, J., & Rosenthal, T. Vicarious and direct counterconditioning of test anxiety through individual and group desensitization. *Behaviour Research and Therapy*, 1969, 7, 359–367.

Mann, L. The effects of emotional role playing on desire to modify smoking habits. *Journal of Experimental and Social Psychology*, 1967, *3*, 334–348.

Mann, L., & Janis, I. A follow-up study on the long-term effects of emotional role playing. *Personality and Social Psychology*, 1968, *8*, 339–342.

Marquis, J. N., & Morgan, W. G. *A guidebook for systematic desensitization*. Palo Alto, California: Veterans' Workshop, 1968.

Marquis, J. N., Morgan, W. G., & Piaget, G. W. *A guidebook for systematic desensitization*. Palo Alto, California: Veterans' Workshop, 1973.

Marks, I., Boulougouris, J., & Marset, P. Flooding versus desensitization in the treatment of phobic patients: A crossover study. *British Journal of Psychiatry*, 1971, *119*, 353–375.

Maupin, E. W. On meditation. In C. T. Tart (Ed.), *Altered states of consciousness*. New York: John Wiley and Sons, 1969, pp. 177–186.

Mealia, W. L., & Nawas, M. M. The comparative effectiveness of systematic desensitization and implosive therapy in the treatment of snake phobia. *Journal of Behavior Therapy and Experimental Psychiatry*, 1971, 2, 85–94.

Meichenbaum, D. H. Therapist manual for cognitive behavior modification. Unpublished, University of Waterloo, Waterloo, Ontario, Canada, 1974.

Meichenbaum, D. H., & Cameron, R. The clinical potential and pitfalls of modifying what clients say to themselves. In M. J. Mahoney & C. E. Thoresen (Eds.), *Self-control: Power to the person*. Monterey, California: Brooks/Cole, 1974.

Merbaum, M. The conditioning of affective self-references by three classes of generalized reinforcers. *Journal of Personality*, 1963, *31*, 179–191.

Meyer, J. B. Strowig, W., & Hosford, R. E. Behavioral-reinforcement counseling with rural high school youth. *Journal of Counseling Psychology*, 1970, *17*, 127–132.

Miller, M. M. Hypnotic-aversion treatment of homosexuality. *Journal of the National Medical Association*, 1963, *55*, 411–415.

Mischel, W. *Personality and assessment.* New York: Wiley, 1968.

Mischel, W. *Introduction to personality.* New York: Holt, Rinehart and Winston, 1971.

Moore, N. Behavior therapy in bronchial asthma: A controlled study. *Journal of Psychosomatic Research*, 1965, *9*, 257–276.

Moreno, J. L. *Psychodrama.* Volume 7. New York: Beacon House, 1946.

Morgan, W. J. Nonnecessary conditions or useful procedures in desensitization: A reply to Wilkins. *Psychological Bulletin*, 1973, *79*, 373–375.

Morganstern, K. P. Implosive therapy and flooding procedures: A critical review. *Psychological Bulletin*, 1973, *79*, 318–334.

Myrick, R. D. Effect of a model on verbal behavior in counseling. *Journal of Counseling Psychology*, 1969, *16*, 185–190.

Nawas, M., Fishman, S., & Pucel, J. A standardized desensitization program applicable to group and individual treatments. *Behaviour Research and Therapy*, 1970, *8*, 49–56.

O'Connor, R. D. Modification of social withdrawal through symbolic modeling. *Journal of Applied Behavior Analysis*, 1969, *7*, 15–22.

Oliveau, D., Agras, W., Leitenberg, H., Moore, R., & Wright, D. Systematic desensitization, therapeutically oriented instructions and selective positive reinforcement. *Behaviour Research and Therapy*, 1969, *7*, 27–33.

O'Neil, D., & Howell, R. Three modes of hierarchy presentation in systematic desensitization therapy, *Behaviour Research and Therapy*, 1969, *7*, 289–294.

Osterhouse, R. A. Desensitization and study-skills training as treatment for two types of test-anxious students. *Journal of Counseling Psychology*, 1972, *19*, 300–306.

Pavlov, I. P. *Conditioned reflexes.* London: Oxford University Press, 1927.

Pavlov, I. P. *Lectures on conditioned reflexes.* New York: International University Press, 1941.

Paul, G. L. *Insight vs. desensitization in psychotherapy.* Stanford, California: Stanford University Press, 1966.

Paul, G. L. Insight vs. desensitization in psychotherapy two years after termination. *Journal of Consulting Psychology*, 1967, *31*, 333–348.

Paul, G. L. Outcome of systematic desensitization I: Background procedures and uncontrolled reports of individual treatment. In C. M. Franks (Ed.), *Behavior therapy: Appraisal and status.* New York: McGraw-Hill, 1969a, pp. 63–104.

Paul, G. L. Outcome of systematic desensitization II: Controlled investigations of individual treatment, technique variations, and current status. In C. M. Franks (Ed.), *Behavior therapy: Appraisal and status.* New York: McGraw-Hill, 1969b, pp. 105–159.

Paul, G. L., & Shannon, D. T. Treatment of anxiety through systematic desensitization in therapy groups. *Journal of Abnormal Psychology,* 1966, *71,* 124.

Paul, G. L., & Trimble, R. W. Recorded vs. "live" relaxation training and hypnotic suggestion: Comparative effectiveness for reducing physiological arousal and inhibiting stress response. *Behavior Therapy,* 1970, *3,* 285–302.

Pepyne, E. The control of interview content through minimal social stimuli. Unpublished doctoral dissertation, Amherst, University of Massachusetts, 1968.

Pepyne, E., & Zimmer, J. Verbal conditioning and the counseling interview. Unpublished paper, Amherst, University of Massachusetts, 1969.

Polin, A. T. The effect of flooding and physical suppression as extinction techniques on an anxiety-motivated avoidance locomotor response. *Journal of Psychology,* 1959, *47,* 253–255.

Prentice, N. M. The influencing of live and symbolic modeling on promoting moral judgment of adolescent delinquents. *Journal of Abnormal Psychology,* 1972, *80,* 157–161.

Prochaska, J. O. Symptom and dynamic cues in the implosive treatment of test anxiety. *Journal of Abnormal Psychology,* 1971, *77,* 133–142.

Rachman, S. Studies in desensitization, II: Flooding. *Behaviour Research and Therapy,* 1966, *4,* 1–6.

Rachman, S. *Phobias; Their nature and control.* Springfield, Illinois: C. C. Thomas, 1968.

Rachman, S. Treatment by prolonged exposure to high intensity stimulation. *Behaviour Research and Therapy,* 1969, *7,* 295–302.

Rachman, S., & Teasdale, J. *Aversion therapy and behaviour disorders: An analysis.* Coral Gables, Florida: University of Miami Press, 1969.

Rathus, S. A. An experimental investigation of assertive training in a group setting. *Journal of Behavior Therapy and Experimental Psychiatry,* 1972, *3,* 81–86.

Rathus, S. A. A 30-item schedule for assessing assertive behavior. *Behavior Therapy,* 1973a, *4,* 398–406.

Rathus, S. A. Instigation of assertive behavior through video-tape mediated assertive models and directed practice. *Behaviour Research and Therapy,* 1973b, *11,* 57–65.

Raymond, M. Case of fetishism treated by aversion therapy. *British Medical Journal,* 1965, *2,* 854–857.

Richardson, F. C., & Suinn, R. M. A comparison of traditional systematic desensitization, accelerated massed desensitization, and anxiety management training in the treatment of mathematics anxiety. *Behavior Therapy,* 1973, *4,* 212–218.

Riddick, C., & Mayer, R. The efficacy of automated relaxation training with response contingent feedback. *Behavior Therapy,* 1973, *3,* 331–337.

Rimm, D. C., & Masters, J. C. *Behavior therapy: Techniques and empirical findings.* New York: Academic Press, 1974.

Risley, T., & Wolf, M. M. Establishing functional speech in echolaic children. *Behaviour Research and Therapy,* 1967, 5, 73–88.

Ritter, B. The group treatment of children's snake phobias using vicarious and contact desensitization procedures. *Behaviour Research and Therapy,* 1968, 6, 1–6.

Rogers, J. M. Operant conditioning in a quasi-therapy setting. *Journal of Abnormal and Social Psychology,* 1960, 60, 247–252.

Rose, S. D. *Treating children in groups.* San Francisco: Jossey-Bass, Inc., 1973.

Ryan, A. T. Reinforcement counseling with small groups in modifying study behavior of college students. Paper presented to American Personnel and Guidance Association Convention. Minneapolis, Minnesota, 1965.

Ryan, A. T. Influence of different cueing procedures on counseling effectiveness. *Proceedings of the 73rd Annual Convention of the American Psychological Association,* 1966, pp. 351–352.

Salter, A. *Conditioned reflex therapy.* New York: Capricorn, 1949.

Salzinger, K. Reinforcement of verbal affect responses of normal subjects during the interview. *Journal of Abnormal and Social Psychology,* 1960, 60, 127–130.

Schmahl, D., Lichtenstein, E., & Harris, D. Successful treatment of habitual smokers with warm, smoky air and rapid smoking. *Journal of Consulting and Clinical Psychology,* 1972, 38, 105–111.

Schroeder, W. W. The effect of reinforcement counseling and model-reinforcement counseling on information-seeking behavior of high school students. Unpublished doctoral dissertation, Stanford University, 1964.

Schubot, E. D. The influence of hypnotic and muscular relaxation in systematic desensitization of phobias. Unpublished doctoral dissertation, Stanford University, 1966.

Scrignar, C., Swanson, W., & Bloom, W. Use of systematic desensitization in the treatment of airplane phobic patients. *Behaviour Research and Therapy,* 1973, 11, 129–131.

Serber, M. Teaching the nonverbal components of assertive training. *Journal of Behavior Therapy and Experimental Psychiatry,* 1972, 3, 179–183.

Shapiro, D., & Birk, L. Group therapy in experimental perspective. *International Journal of Group Psychotherapy,* 1967, 17, 211–224.

Shaw, D. W., & Thoresen, C. E. Effects of modeling and desensitization in reducing dentist phobia. *Journal of Counseling Psychology,* 1974, 21, 415–420.

Sherman, A. R., & Plummer, I. L. Training in relaxation as a behavioral self-management skill: An exploratory investigation. *Behavior Therapy,* 1973, *4,* 543–550.

Sherman, T. M., & Cormier, W. H. The use of subjective scales for measuring interpersonal reactions. *Journal of Behavior Therapy and Experimental Psychiatry,* 1972, *3,* 279–280.

Shoben, E. J. Psychotherapy as a problem in learning theory. *Psychological Bulletin,* 1949, *46,* 366–392.

Sidman, M. *Tactics of scientific research: Evaluating experimental data in psychology.* New York: Basic Books, 1960.

Smith, E. W. L. Postural and gestural communication of A and B "therapist types" during dyadic interviews. *Journal of Consulting and Clinical Psychology,* 1972, *39,* 29–36.

Smith, J. A., & Lewis, W. A. Effects of videotaped models on the communications of college students in counseling. *Journal of Counseling Psychology,* 1974, *21,* 78–80.

Staats, A. W. Language behavior therapy: A derivative of social behaviorism. *Behavior Therapy,* 1972, *3,* 165–192.

Stampfl, T. G., & Levis, D. J. Essentials of implosive therapy: A learning-theory-based psychodynamic behavioral therapy. *Journal of Abnormal Psychology,* 1967, *73,* 496–503.

Stampfl, T. G. Implosive therapy — a behavioral therapy? *Behaviour Research and Therapy,* 1968, *6,* 31–36.

Staub, E. Duration of stimulus explosure as determinant of the efficacy of flooding procedures in the elimination of fear. *Behaviour Research and Therapy,* 1968, *6,* 131–132.

Staub, E. Fantasy, self-preservation, and the reinforcing power of groups. In P. S. Houts and M. Serber (Eds.), *After the turn on, what?* Champaign, Illinois: Research Press, 1972, 45–60.

Stilwell, W. E., & Thoresen, C. E. Effects of social modeling on vocational behaviors of Mexican-American and non-Mexican-American adolescents. *Vocational Guidance Quarterly,* 1972, *20,* 279–286.

Stolz, S. B. Overview of NIMH support of research in behavior therapy. *Journal of Applied Behavior Analysis,* 1973, *6,* 509–512.

Suinn, R. M., Edie, C. A., & Spinelli, P. R. Accelerated massed desensitization: Innovation in short-term treatment. *Behavior Therapy,* 1970, *3,* 303–311.

Suinn, R. M., & Richardson, I. Anxiety management training: A nonspecific behavior therapy program for anxiety control. *Behavior Therapy,* 1971, *2,* 498–510.

Thomas, E. J., Walter, C. L., & O'Flaherty, K. A verbal problem checklist for use in assessing family verbal behavior. *Behavior Therapy,* 1974, *5,* 215–221.

Thoresen, C. E. An experimental comparison of counseling techniques for producing information-seeking behavior. Unpublished doctoral dissertation, Stanford University, 1964.

Thoresen, C. E. Behavioral counseling: An introduction. *The School Counselor*, 1966, *14*, 13–21.

Thoresen, C. E. Comment to C. A. Mahler, Group counseling. *The Personnel and Guidance Journal*, 1971, 49, 608–610.

Thoresen, C. E. Training behavioral counselors. In F. W. Clark, D. R. Evans, and L. A. Hamerlynck (Eds.), *Implementing behavioral programs for schools and clinics*. Champaign, Illinois: Research Press, 1972.

Thoresen, C. E., Krumboltz, J. D., & Varenhorst, B. B. The sex factor in model-reinforcement counseling. *Proceedings of the 73rd Annual Convention of the American Psychological Association*, 1965, pp. 349–350.

Thoresen, C. E., Krumboltz, J. D., & Varenhorst, B. B. Sex of counselors and models: Effect on client career exploration. *Journal of Counseling Psychology*, 1967, *14*, 503–508.

Thoresen, C. E., & Krumboltz, J. D. Similarity of social models and clients in behavioral counseling: Two experimental studies. *Journal of Counseling Psychology*, 1968, *15*, 393–401.

Thoresen, C. E., & Hamilton, J. A. Peer social modeling in promoting career behaviors. *Vocational Guidance Quarterly*, 1972, *20*, 210–216.

Thoresen, C. E., & Hosford, R. Behavioral approaches to counseling. In C. E. Thoresen (Ed.), *Behavior modification in education*. Seventy-second Yearbook of the National Society for the Study of Education. Chicago: University of Chicago Press, 1973.

Tilley, D. P. Counseling theory and behavior: A rating and factor analysis. Unpublished doctoral dissertation, University of California, Santa Barbara, 1972.

Turk, D. Cognitive modification of pain. Unpublished, University of Waterloo, Waterloo, Ontario, Canada, 1974.

Valins, S., & Ray, A. Effects of cognitive desensitization on avoidance behavior. *Journal of Personality and Social Psychology*, 1967, *7*, 345–350.

Varenhorst, B. B. An experimental comparison of nonverbal factors determining reinforcement effectiveness of model-reinforcement counseling. Unpublished doctoral dissertation, Stanford University, 1964.

Varenhorst, B. B. Behavioral group counseling. In G. M. Gazda (Ed.), *Theories and methods of group counseling in the schools*. Springfield, Illinois: C. C. Thomas, 1969, pp. 119–156.

Ventis, W. Case history: The use of laughter as an alternative response in systematic desensitization. *Behavior Therapy*, 1973, *7*, 120–122.

Verplanck, W. S. The control of the content of conversation: Reinforcement of statements of opinion. *Journal of Abnormal and Social Psychology*, 1955, *55*, 668–676.

Wahler, R. G., & Cormier, W. H. The ecological interview: A first step in out-patient child behavior therapy. *Journal of Behavior Therapy and Experimental Psychiatry*, 1970, *1*, 279–289.

Wallace, C. J., Davis, J. R., Liberman, R. P., & Baker, V. Modeling and staff behavior. *Journal of Consulting and Clinical Psychology*, 1973, *41*, 426–433.

Walters, R. H., Leat, M., & Mezei, L. Inhibition and disinhibition of responses to empathetic learning. *Canadian Journal of Psychology*, 1963, *17*, 235–243.

Waskow, I. E. Reinforcement in a therapy-like situation through selective responding to feelings or content. *Journal of Consulting Psychology*, 1962, *26*, 11–19.

Watson, J. B., & Rayner, R. Conditioned emotional reaction. *Journal of Experimental Psychology*, 1920, *3*, 1–4.

Watson, J. P., & Marks, I. M. Relevant and irrelevant fear in flooding — a crossover study of phobic patients. *Behavior Therapy*, 1971, *2*, 275–293.

Watts, F. N. Desensitization as an habituation phenomenon: I. Stimulus intensity as a determinant of the effects of stimulus lengths. *Behaviour Research and Therapy*, 1973, *9*, 209–217.

Watts, F. N. The control of spontaneous recovery of anxiety in imaginal desensitization. *Behaviour Research and Therapy*, 1974, *12*, 57–59.

Weil, G., & Goldfried, M. R. Treatment of insomnia in an eleven-year-old child through self-relaxation. *Behavior Therapy*, 1973, *4*, 282–294.

Whalen, C. Effects of a model and instructions on group verbal behaviors. *Journal of Consulting and Clinical Psychology*, 1969, *33*, 509–521.

Wheeler, L., & Caggiula, A. R. The contagion of aggression. *Journal of Experimental Social Psychology*, 1966, *2*, 1–10.

Wilkins, W. Desensitization: Social and cognitive factors underlying the effectiveness of Wolpe's procedure. *Psychological Bulletin*, 1971, *76*, 311–317.

Willis, R. W., & Edwards, J. A. A study of the comparative effectiveness of systematic desensitization and implosive therapy. *Behaviour Research and Therapy*, 1969, *7*, 387–395.

Wilson, F. W., & Walters, R. H. Modification of speech output of near-mute schizophrenics through social-learning procedures. *Behaviour Research and Therapy*, 1966, *4*, 59–67.

Wilson, G. D. Efficacy of "flooding" procedures in desensitization of fear: A theoretical note. *Behaviour Research and Therapy*, 1967, *5*, 138.

Wilson, G. T. Innovations in the modification of phobic behaviors in two clinical cases. *Behavior Therapy*, 1973, *3*, 426–430.

Wolpe, J. *Psychotherapy by reciprocal inhibition*. Stanford: Stanford University Press, 1958.

Wolpe, J. The systematic desensitization treatment of neuroses. *Journal of Nervous and Mental Disease*, 1961, *132*, 189–203.

Wolpe, J. Conditioned inhibition of craving in drug addiction: A pilot experiment. *Behaviour Research and Therapy*, 1965, *2*, 285–288.

Wolpe, J. *The practice of behavior therapy.* New York: Pergamon Press, 1969.

Wolpe, J., & Lang, P. J. A fear survey schedule for use in behavior therapy. *Behaviour Research and Therapy,* 1964, *2,* 27–30.

Wolpe, J., & Lazarus, A. A. *Behavior therapy techniques.* New York: Pergamon Press, 1966.

Wright, B. Aversive conditioning of self-induced seizures. *Behavior Therapy,* 1973, *4,* 712–713.

Yates, A. J. *Behavior therapy.* New York: John Wiley and Sons, 1970.

Zimmer, J. M., & Park, P. Factor analysis of counselor communications. *Journal of Counseling Psychology,* 1967, *14,* 198–203.

Zimmer, J. M., & Anderson, S. Dimensions of positive regard and empathy. *Journal of Counseling Psychology,* 1968, *15,* 417–426.

Zimmer, J. M., Wightman, L. E., & McArthur, D. L. Categories of counselor behavior as defined from cross validated factor stuctures. Final Report, United States Office of Education Project No. 9-A0003. University of Massachusetts, School of Education, Amherst, Massachusetts, 1970.

Zimmer, J. M., & Pepyne, E. W. A descriptive and comparative study of dimensions of counselor response. *Journal of Counseling Psychology,* 1971, *18,* 441–447.

INDEX